HARDCORE

Dedicated to Walter, Rosa, James, Callum, Marley, Elfyn and Sonny

On the front cover: Photographs © Paul Burgess
On the back cover: Photographs © Paul Burgess; arrangement
and graphics by Louise Colbourne.

This edition published in the United Kingdom in 2023 by
Thames & Hudson Ltd, 181A High Holborn, London WC1V 7QX

This edition published in the United States of America in 2023 by
Thames & Hudson Inc., 500 Fifth Avenue, New York, New York 10110

Interior layout designed by Louise Colbourne

British Library Cataloguing-in-Publication Data
A catalogue record for this book is available
from the British Library

Library of Congress Control Number 2023936968

ISBN 978-0-500-02698-4

Printed in China by RR Donnelley

MIX
Paper | Supporting
responsible forestry
FSC® C144853

Be the first to know about our new releases,
exclusive content and author events by visiting
thamesandhudson.com
thamesandhudsonusa.com
thamesandhudson.com.au

HARDCORE

The Cinematic World of PULP

PAUL BURGESS

LOUISE COLBOURNE

PRELUDE

Paul Burgess and Louise Colbourne

This Is Hardcore is Pulp's cry for help. Inspired by Jarvis Cocker's disgust for the fame he'd sought since childhood cruelly letting him down, Hardcore remains their greatest artistic achievement to date. A giant, sprawling, beautiful, and beautifully flawed masterpiece of an album, that tackled some of the most inappropriately grown-up issues of the day – fame, ageing, mortality, drugs, pornography, and pornography-as-a-metaphor-for-fame-and-success – This Is Hardcore is the most exquisitely realized record of the 1990s – bar none. I love it to bits, and I don't care who knows it.

Jane Savidge. Writer, former Pulp PR with Savage and Best.

This book seeks to evoke a sense of film noir, a cinematic journey to reveal the seductive and sometimes darker mood that prevailed for many when the last century came to its giddy climax toward the end of the 1990s. Twenty-five years have passed since Paul Burgess packed his boxes of photographs and the video footage he took of Pulp during the *This Is Hardcore* period away into storage. Now many of these photographs are being seen for the first time – vivid, grainy, effervescent images of Pulp both in front of the camera and behind the curtains.

This opening section sets the scene for the unfolding contents of the book. In 'The Photographs', Paul talks of the inspiration that led him to work with Pulp and his thoughts looking back on the album. Louise Colbourne coordinated the contributions by other artists and writers, and in 'The Book' she talks about the idea of creating a container for holding stories with on-going possibilities. In 'The Apartment', Peter Saville explains how the photographs for the *This Is Hardcore* album cover materialized. Finally, an essay by Stephen Mallinder, 'Wide-Eyed and Gleadless', eloquently describes the atmosphere of the album. Stephen also reflects on growing up in Sheffield, an experience both he and Jarvis Cocker shared, and the parallel paths they took since leaving the city that helped to shape their lives.

Steve Mackey, Paul Burgess and Jarvis Cocker.
Photograph by Jeannette Lee (1998).

THE PHOTOGRAPHS

Paul Burgess

Imagine a pile of dusty boxes, kept in the dark for twenty-five years. These boxes contain photographs and videos made on an unforgettable journey with a group called Pulp. Six years spent documenting music video shoots, live gigs, parties and special events, many of them based around the sixth Pulp album *This Is Hardcore*, released in March 1998. Photographs lying in wait within these cardboard walls – a Fujichrome time capsule resurfacing from a unique period in my life.

You might be wondering how I came to take these pictures? I first saw Pulp live in 1994 and, like many others, I was captivated. The rapport Jarvis had with his audience reminded me of the connection made between band and audience during punk gigs of the late 1970s. They had that spark, that indescribable 'thing' and the live performances were riveting, incorporating the intrigue and intelligence of both the art and film worlds. I wanted to get involved.

Inspired by Jarvis Cocker's clarion call from the stage at Glastonbury:

'If you want something to happen enough, then it will actually happen, ok?
So, if a lanky get like me can do it, and us lot, you can do it too'.

I decided to take him up on his advice.

In January 1996, I approached Jarvis and asked if I could design some visual promotional material for the band. I wrote a letter and put it into a battered box-file alongside examples of my work – 1970s space bubble gum cards, ideas for T-shirt designs, and some over-excited proposals for 'Pulp Merchandise' – a Pulp View-Master set, amongst others. I heard nothing for a few weeks and then I got a call from Jeannette Lee, the group's manager, asking me to come into the office. Jarvis had enjoyed my box of 'special things' and, as it turned out, we shared similar artistic reference points. First, they asked me to design an official Pulp 1997 calendar. I usually work with photomontage and, so, decided to piece together twelve images, one for each month, using 3D-box art, staged environments and collages of cutouts from photographs. Everyone seemed happy with the end result.

Around this time, I asked Pulp if I could photograph any events they had coming up, and between 1995 and 2001, I documented – using photography, collage and video footage – live concerts, video shoots, launch parties, DJ sets and anything else out of the blue. I even photographed Jarvis's yellow Hillman Imp being crushed in a scrapyard ahead of being given away as a competition prize. Mister, we just want your car.

I had a cheap-and-cheerful DIY approach, using a Lomo camera, an old Pentax SLR, a plastic 3D camera and anything else I could afford at the time. Those years started with behind-the-scenes shots during the video shoot for 'Mis-Shapes' at the Hammersmith Palais – where I arrived with my camera but somehow ended up as an extra in the first scene, on the dancefloor – and they concluded with the 'We Love Life' tour. The release of *This Is Hardcore* lead to the creation of four major music videos and I was lucky enough to be there, with my camera, for all of them.

The most memorable shoot involved a week on the set of the 'This Is Hardcore' video, at Pinewood Studios, in February 1998. During this more extended period, I began to have conversations with all five members of Pulp. I discovered that not only Jarvis but also Mark Webber and Steve Mackey had a real interest in photography and the moving image. At a time before digital cameras or camera phones were available to the mass market, film was something you 'shot' and photographs were something that could be 'held' in your hand or kept in a photo album. All the photographs you will find in this book were taken on 35mm film, in the last years of the predominantly analogue era. The internet was a new thing, the words 'social media' didn't mean anything to anyone and, besides some test Polaroids taken by Doug Nichol, there was not a clamour for this kind of behind-the-scenes photography on music-video shoots. Encouraged by Jeannette, I was given the creative freedom to document intimate moments, as well as public ones, and to capture scenarios that would otherwise have been overlooked or forgotten.

Speaking in terms of Pulp's music, if *Different Class* (1995) was the celebration party, then *This Is Hardcore* was the come down, the morning after, the soul-searching feeling you get when you have done something bad the night before but can't quite remember what it was. The photographic images I made during this period reflect the existentialist, blurry and kaleidoscopic experimentalism of the album Pulp had created and the world that grew to surround it.

Like Scott Walker after the Walker Brothers, like Bowie once he got to Berlin, *This Is Hardcore* shows Pulp pushing the boundaries of everything they had done before. The ten-minute drone at the end of 'The Day After the Revolution' cleanses the palate, opening the way for a new era of Pulp, and the opus of a music video provided by the title track is just breathtaking. Taking into consideration the addition of some of the B-sides and demo tracks recorded at this time, 'It's a Dirty World', 'The Professional', 'That Boy's Evil', 'Ladies Man' and 'My Erection', which explore the use of sampling, loops, vocoder, loungecore and electro beats; this is Pulp at their most progressive.

This Is Hardcore is an album made by a group ready to face its demons – personal, professional or otherwise. Many find the album dark; some find it sexually charged, others find it life-affirming. Maybe it is all of these and more?

I hope you will open the pages of this book and feel something of how I felt when I opened those dusty boxes of photographs from another time in my life. Perhaps this book will bring nostalgia, or maybe an entirely fresh perspective on a group who are, by now, so embedded into our cultural consciousness. Most of all, I hope that the story of how these photographs came into existence, and the processes of expression they depict, act as a catalyst for more creativity in the future.

Welcome to the *Hardcore* life...

Above:
Abstracted (one hundred frames) (2012),
Louise Colbourne, 35mm film still

THE BOOK

Louise Colbourne

'They're stories within stories [...] the pictures became strange pieces of fiction.' Dianne Keaton (1983)[1]

Containing a fusion of photography, music, art, film and memories of the group Pulp, this book holds *stories within stories* that fold in and overlap the lives and times of many of the artists that are presented within it. The title of the book *Hardcore* has a meaning for us beyond the intentions of its original inclusion in the album title *This Is Hardcore*. For Jarvis, the title spoke about the need to strip things back to the core, 'taking it all the way down to the marrowbone'[2], and to reflect his observations about fame and hardcore pornography. For this book, the definition of 'hardcore' that we are referring to sums up the commitment and dedication Paul Burgess had toward the group Pulp when he documented their work all those years ago. It is this kind of hardcore enthusiasm that can be found in abundance throughout this book.

   Hardcore can be seen as a collection of memories, an exhibition of artworks, a story about the *This Is Hardcore* journey, or all these things combined. The photographs, collages and video stills herein are arranged according to four of the songs from the *This Is Hardcore* album: 'This Is Hardcore', 'Help the Aged', 'A Little Soul' and 'Party Hard'. Ursula K. Le Guin wrote that books hold things as well as words and they may be seen 'as necessary elements of a whole which itself cannot be characterized either as conflict or as harmony, since its purpose is neither resolution nor stasis but continuing process'[3]. In other words, books can act as containers for an ongoing and everchanging stream of thoughts, objects, feelings and interpretations. It is in this way that we came to see *Hardcore* as a container – something that could be rifled through, its contents discovered and the feelings the book elicits surprising and unique to every person who opens it. A good illustration of this was an action taken by Jarvis Cocker in 2022 at the launch events for his book, *Good Pop, Bad Pop*, when he brought a plastic bag onto the stage – filled with artifacts from his attic. Jarvis's bag contained items that acted as signposts from the past that direct toward the creation and artistic concept of Pulp.

   Like the many boxes of archival material belonging to Paul Burgess, or the box of items that Paul sent to Jeannette Lee and Jarvis to ask if he could work with them, the idea of a box has come to be synonymous with this book, representing the meticulous act of collecting fragments from past worlds to create stories for the future – a preoccupation both Jarvis and Paul seem to share. Much like the artist John Stezaker, Jarvis's tutor on the film and video course he attended at (Central) St Martin's School of Art between 1988–1991, Paul and Jarvis have a fascination with the images and objects from the era in which they were born and grew up.

1   Keaton, D. and Heiferman, M. *Still life*. New York: Callaway, 1983, p.1–3.
2   The back of the 'This Is Hardcore' single promo sleeve.
3   Le Guin, Ursula K., *The Carrier Bag Theory of Fiction*, INOTA Books, 2020, p.35.

Paul's eye for detail, and fondness for the tangibility of objects and ephemera, enabled him to photograph incidental, intimate moments with Pulp, focusing on the band members' shoes or hands or general dressing-room detritus. He also collected discarded items from the film and video sets – production notes, polaroid photographs and storyboard sketches – often found in the dustbin on set. The work of 'curation' here is as much to do with 'taking care' of fragments as it is to frame and create space for groups of more major work.

Another container, with which we are familiar, is the film canister. Like a film canister, which contains edits and outtakes from the cutting-room floor, a book is the container for material to be arranged and edited in a similar way to create something new, the container that frames the narrative. The *This Is Hardcore* album itself is cinematic in its nature, particularly the music video for the title track, in which the director, Doug Nichol, tells a story of fame and excess through a plot he devised using classic Hollywood tropes rendered on vivid technicolour film.

When making a book, it is easy to fall into a habit of simply describing its contents. However, it is also an important part of the author's job to weave the details into a story. So, rather than stating exactly what it was like then, or what happened at any given moment in time, we have collected here a range of contributors to impart a reflective narrative of the *This Is Hardcore* period. Reproductions of paintings, photographs and written memoirs are placed alongside Paul's previously unseen photographs and our collages, to create new and possibly – to use Diane Keaton's words – 'strange pieces of fiction' for readers to unearth twenty-five years on.

The Ukrainian-Danish artist Sergei Sviatchenko has contributed bold and ambiguous portraits from his *Less* collage series for the 'This Is Hardcore' chapter using a selection of Paul's photographs taken at Pinewood Studios. Sviatchenko's minimal use just two or three elements is echoed by John Stezaker's collages, which also feature in the 'This Is Hardcore' chapter. Stezaker's collages often artfully use just one image that is then subjected to one action such as a cut, and for this chapter the subjects and arrangements of the images reflect the filmic quality of the song.

The 'Help the Aged' chapter features the image of an ink drawing by American artist John Currin, called *The Neverending Story* (1994). Jarvis had been drawn to Currin's work, he could see links between his paintings and the themes about ageing in the song. Jarvis was also impressed by the passionate and quirky attitude of the film maker Florian Habicht, which led to the commissioning of the film *Pulp: A Film About Life, Death & Supermarkets* (2014). For this chapter we have included an amusing account of Florian's experiences making the film in Sheffield. The film is a documentation of a concert given by Pulp when they re-formed in 2012, and it also acts as a touching portrait of the people of the city of Sheffield. To add further to the vivid accounts of times spent with Pulp, we have a welcome contribution by the DJ and art curator Martin Green in the 'Party Hard' chapter. Martin offers a window into the London club scene in the 1990s and in particular the Smashing club nights that hold so many memories for the regular Friday night visitors, including members of Pulp.

As Donna Harraway states 'it matters what stories we tell to tell other stories with'[4] and a key contribution included in this book comes in the form of a recent conversation between Paul and Candida Doyle, Pulp's keyboard player. In the 'A Little Soul' chapter, Candida talks openly and honestly about the *This Is Hardcore* period, pointing out that the actual experience did not look and feel as good as it may appear now. Paul and Candida discuss the controversy surrounding the photograph used for the album cover, the portrait of the young model Ksenia Zlobina, amongst other more personal subjects such as mental health. Candida's story shines a light on the darker side to fame and glamour in the 1990s, which the album aims to portray with such relevance. Much like the *fin de siècle* of the previous century, this story could be heralding the closure of one type of narrative trope to make way for the beginning of the hope for a more enlightened era in the new millennium.

    Hardcore contains fragments of lived experiences, of times remembered and times best forgotten, good times and heavy times. Pulp fans will desire truth and beauty in this book, but we hope it is reflective of more than just the representations of certain people, places and events. Much like music that passes through an infinite mixture of re-appropriated renditions to be experienced anew, each re-telling emphasizes nostalgic elements, as well as contemporary experiences. This book aims to be a polyphonic arrangement of memories, images, songs and relationships.

4   Le Guin, Ursula K., *The Carrier Bag Theory of Fiction*, INOTA Books, 2020, p. 10.

THE APARTMENT

Peter Saville, London 2022

In the mid-1990s I lived in an apartment on Hill Street in Mayfair, London. The place, known as 'The Apartment', also functioned as my studio. The interior was refurbished in collaboration with my friend, the interior architect Ben Kelly, who had also designed The Haçienda's interior for Factory Records. 'The Apartment' style could be described as 'neo 1970s'. Many of the young artists in London at the time were intrigued to visit and meet me there. Consequently, at times the place became something of a salon. This 'residency' was supported by my associate Mike Meiré of Meiré und Meiré, an independent creative consultancy based in Cologne.

Jarvis, who I didn't know personally, saw 'The Apartment' in a magazine and called me to say he had a project he'd like to discuss. He explained he was collaborating with the artist John Currin on the artwork for Pulp's upcoming album *This Is Hardcore*. He thought I may be able to help bring their vision to life. I knew of John and, when discussing the project, he and I soon established a fluency between ourselves, identifying references, specifically material of an 'adult nature', which we'd share in order to define the type of image we wanted to achieve. Around that time, I had been working with the photographer Horst Diekgerdes and I felt his lens may be a powerful way to translate the feeling and atmosphere we envisaged for the cover. Horst agreed to join the project and locations were chosen, principally 'The Apartment' and the London Hilton hotel, on Park Lane, which was a stylistic time capsule and, in that sense, a readymade set.

It was a great team to work with – Jarvis, John and Horst. The eroticism of the cover was something I didn't often indulge, but it was in a way a fantasy realization of the Mayfair apartment.

With the campaign material for the album, when it came to ads on the side of double-decker buses, Transport for London were prepared to accept the album image alone on a bus and they were prepared to accept solely the title *This Is Hardcore* – but they were not prepared to accept the image and the title together!

One of the tasks in designing the sleeve was to combine Horst's photos from the two locations of the photo shoot – to help the flow and to tell a single story. Because John Currin was an artist, I hoped this unification could also make the photos look evocative of paintings.

I altered the photos in Photoshop, giving them a digital painterly effect. Trying it on the cover image, the result on Ksenia's hair was stunning. I knew then we could use this technique to unify them all.

Howard Wakefield, Colour & Form Ltd, 2022

Photograph by Horst Diekgerdes.
Design by Howard Wakefield and Paul Hetherington.
Art Direction by John Currin and Peter Saville.
Casting by Sascha Behrendt.
Styling by Camille Bidault-Waddington.

WIDE-EYED AND GLEADLESS

Stephen Mallinder

This is hardcore, and so it became known. An unapologetic and incandescent light turned on at the party's end. We thought ourselves beautiful, soft toned and erudite, but we looked like cheap wedding cakes in the blinding light of a new day.

Viewing it now, from decades into the future, as I did the first time round but from another hemisphere, through the wrong end of a telescope. A fragmented, partially remembered, world; feelings hazily recalled but visually rendered in perfect microscopic detail. Optimistic, but disintegrating, memories collected from the chemists in packs of Kodachrome opening up in celluloid grain. A Ken Loach film we think we might have watched, shot in lustful, but not quite real, Pantone. A dislocated northern world repositioned to a cosmopolitan place and time.

Images created to spotlight an album of slowly unfurling beauty. A barbed wire curio clenched in a velvet glove. The beauty is caught deep within its blossoming seed. Chris Thomas's pitch-perfect production, songcraft of the highest order bathed in lush Barryesque strings. All conjuring up hot-night-out-in-the-West-End with the electronic cold wave snapping at its heels. An accompanying epic soundtrack for a poppers comedown. A blunt and unremorseful morning-after holler, sprawling on a burst couch. Uncertain, a messiah inversion, questioning manhood on a fucked-up new day.

Hardcore sentiments with shameless honesty. A k-hole fever dream washed up on a gravel beach, trying to get our bearings; soothed by waves of Nurofen and Lucozade. The class of Teddy Bass, a murky affair but with true intensions, like polyester dreaming of shot silk. Welcome to the new *nouvelle vague* capturing the atrophy of 90s hysterical glamour in granular detail: a very new reality. From Myers Grove, to Ladbroke Grove, a long journey home – skin tones bathed in fluorescent candour on the Circle Line – kitchen-sink modernity.

Something good must come of all this. A world on its millennial turn, an impending future still very speculative, all trying to make personal sense. Start by rifling through the wreckage in the scrub. Find truth in the hinterland: cigarette butts, roaches and crisp packets scattered in a new-reality dream. Find the beauty. It's growing in the street, right up through the concrete, a rose in Shoreditch Harlem.

Although I flatter myself to think so, and I'm sure this is not reciprocated, I often see myself twinned with Pulp, and Jarvis. A bit like towns and cities become inexplicably fraternal with places you've never really heard of: Rotherham twinned with Saint-Quentin in France; Cleethorpes with Königswinter in Germany. Like those towns we share common features, although are rarely in the same place, moving in overlapping but different orbits, occasionally intersecting at events or locations, but mostly bumping into each other in print. Both Sheffield born and raised, less than a decade apart, but emerging in the heady days of punk, this time differential was significant. I, or using the collective pronoun of we in that Cabaret Voltaire functioned as a multi-headed beast, began to take shape before punk, Jarvis and Pulp were a direct response to those seismic times. Both legacies of a world

infused by the likes of arthouse cinema, iconic television, discarded fashion, David Bowie, and, in our case, Brian Eno. We passed on a cultural baton to them. They ran faster than us with it. We breathed the same smog and air, walked the same rain-slicked pavements, hovered over half-pints of bitter in the same West Street pubs, interacted with the weird and wonderful Sheffield nighttime characters. We trod the same carpets that acted as stages in pubs like The Hallamshire, wandered aimlessly around town, inevitably drawn to the, now filled in, 'Hole in the Road' that became the city's epicentre, its infamous urban fishtank that boasted an actual piranha. Perhaps coming from Sheffield we all feel we share a common cause, a reality kinship. In truth, everyone who has ever made music and comes from the city seems to be, at most, within two degrees of separation. I've been around a bit longer so seem to share atoms with almost everyone who has ever hollered into a microphone, twiddled a knob, or dressed up as a complete tool in the cause of performance art. I have I hope, like Pulp, projected the same ideal of 'art as transformation', authentic pop culture, and strange otherness that making music affords us without ever losing sight of what we are, or where we come from.

There is also a parallel path in that, like Jarvis, I had some wanderlust, a need to keep shifting forward. Occasional lapsed northerners. Moving to other cities and parts of the world but never actually becoming completely detached, always connected to the city and its surroundings by some invisible bungee cord. Shifting from the microcosm of Sheffield, relocating, finding new places, unearthing other slightly more exotic bits and bobs, transferring our northern sensibilities to unknown worlds but never really losing the sense of who, and what, we are and where we're from. Moving along, but always keeping a grip on the past with an Adidas bag, or bin bag, full of memorabilia, cultural detritus, real or in your head. Growing up in a meaningful way. Making records is such a wonderful mechanism for capturing ourselves, the times and places we pass through. The immediacy of music can grasp these moments. Even if no one hears what we create, being able to make sense of everything through making and translating it into something to share, is a gift we all have the capacity for. Pulp and Jarvis have demystified this process, encouraging the possible – the art of making the prosaic, the everyday event, meaningful. More than any other band or artist, they have shown us how to grow up, mark time and capture the ever-changing moment stylishly more than any other. Moved and transformed before our eyes, they have been self-deprecating, funny, dark, honest and uncertain. Sometimes taking the piss, always taking the past and our core personality with us wherever we go.

To be fair, most of Pulp's big bits happened when I was actually somewhere else. I watched from a distance with fascination, and some amusement, as the band moved into wider public consciousness. They had always been a name that seemed to appear everywhere in the early post-punk days, working relentlessly in the pubs and clubs of Sheffield. A ubiquitous name on a Xeroxed flyer, a brightly coloured stain on the carpet, not getting noticeably bigger but stubborn and impossible to remove. Although in the intervening years Jarvis himself polished his art credentials and wider perception – he made the cheeky video for Sweet Exorcist's 'Testone', which I loved. While Richard and myself, as Cabaret Voltaire, moved deeper into techno and house music, Pulp were carefully sharpening their pop-cultural, and smart-word, tools. As we became part of some obscure international electronic syndicate, Pulp recalibrated their national, and generational, sensibilities. The result was an unexpected, and perhaps unintended, glittery end of the disco, the voice of a post-rave generation.

Although Pulp's concerted attack on the cultural establishment was well under way while I was living in London, and commuting to Sheffield, I saw much of it through the wrong end of 'the telescope at the other side of the world'. Bemused from afar, watching Pulp dissect pop culture with humour, empathy and brute honesty while living in Australia, as far away as I could possibly be. Although, thankfully, Jarvis popped over down under with two of my music friends, Winnie and Pipes, and said hello while I served time making music and my own culture in the hot desert. I do remember, and did appreciate it – thanks for sitting uncomfortably in a DJ booth in Perth with me while everyone gawped. Regardless of the tyranny of distance, it was an eye opener to see the phenomena that Pulp and Jarvis had become in my absence. From the band impressively riding a wave of thinly disguised optimism and shaky hedonism, *This Is Hardcore* represented the reality, and impact, of that rupture of pop culture. There was a genuine tear of Sheffield pride for me in witnessing what had actually happened following the hardworking days of what I'll call photocopy Pulp. The band although not really becoming part of, but becoming inevitably linked to, the late 90s collision of new confident British music and the too brief, giddy, hopes of a Labour government. When viewed from another part of the world it was frankly weird. This wide-spectrum musical onslaught of an all pervasive drum and bass, a brash two-finger pop salute, and the massed dayglow Gatecrasher hordes, this explosion seemed illusionary. It felt like cultural space dust, that stuff that pops and explodes in your mouth before quickly disappearing to nothingness, sugared poppers, a blurred memory of something that might have happened, but you're not quite sure and you're left with a headache. Pulp stood outside this British pop vector, if not smug then certainly knowing and smarter. *Hardcore* anchored that false-rush experience and tied it down to a more concrete truth. Even if it wore its colours brightly and stylishly, the oily stains remained. It was part of the party, but it was something else altogether.

This Is Hardcore remains, to use the regional vernacular, a proper album. Edged and detailed, noisy and sublime, etched with words that confess the let down, the beauty of the real, pearls and swine. Worried but grown-up and proud. An actual record. We have to accept that music is now a convenience, a utility like gas and water – although we seem to be struggling with these so I am cautious of being patronising here – we switch it on like a Hoover, it sedates and invigorates us accordingly, an invisible ambience to cushion our daily lives, sonic Xanax. So how do we understand music like this? I don't think *This Is Hardcore* was designed as 'music to accompany having your nails done' but maybe, and very ironically, it works well like that. Regardless, if it did, then it would today most likely appear fragmented, as individual tracks on the 'Now That's What I Call Nail Bar' playlist series. It seems so important now to acknowledge the idea of the album, an artist's own sequencing of music, a considered story told with thought. It connects audience and listener, the process of making and creating with the experience of listening and absorbing. Albums give context and meaning, we can stare back into the writer's eyes, follow a train of thought, make connections, rebuke or relate. We can hold the object, turn it in our hands, smudge the cover or wonder if we've misplaced the inner sleeve, look at the credits, laugh at the typos and figure out what mastering means. We wonder at the artwork and make judgements on whether the videos for the singles made sense of what the album tried to portray. We can feel the ghosts of those who made the record tingle through our fingers. All things which now seem lost in the podcast era, all information but little substance, all reference and no ambivalence. Put bluntly, this cultural fragmentation means the album is no longer distilled, even obliquely, into a single package. Music is now deconstructed like a designer meal, we are required to build it ourselves. We retro-engineer all the broken, dispersed parts and see if we can make sense of it. I'm guessing most of us, if we bother to rebuild the parts at all, end up with a broken Lego figure, a hollowed-out musical Frankenstein.

What you are holding in your hands celebrates *This Is Hardcore* as a single entity, a moment in time, a collection of thoughts, ideas and fucked up understandings of the real world being experienced – rather than fleeting, disconnected sounds lost in the mass of the digital ether. Beautiful, lipstick smeared, brash, confident, regretful, a bit whiffy and human.

THIS IS HARDCORE

Production Company: Partizan Midi-Minuit
Director: Doug Nichol
Shoot Date: 9–13th February 1998
Location: L Stage and C Stage, Pinewood Studios,
Pinewood Road, Iver, Bucks, SL0 0NH, England

The music video for 'This Is Hardcore', the title track of the album, was filmed at Pinewood Studios over the course of five days in February 1998. This video is unquestionably the most epic promo video by Pulp. Director Doug Nichol chose a metaphorical direction, through a linked series of set pieces: a 'Sam Spade' private investigator's office, mid-century modern Hollywood melodramas, a stuntman fistfight while Nick tends the bar at a swanky cocktail party and, finally, the eye of the storm leads us to Busby Berkeley-inspired dancers performing a 'flower scene' on a giant revolving turntable.

Douglas Sirk's *Written on the Wind* pervades the atmosphere. Doug Nichol stands on set in a world of blue feather boas and gold-clad dancing women. People occupy the space like ornate pieces of furniture: Tracey Emin on set, on the bed – but not that bed. On Thursday evening we watch *Top of the Pops* in the dressing room – members of Pulp strewn around alongside the clothes, the shoes, a strange Japanese toy bird, a gift from a fan. During a tea break, Jarvis dances to 'The Message' while, on the adjacent stage at Pinewood Studios, Stanley Kubrick films *Eyes Wide Shut* behind closed doors.

'This Is Hardcore' is a fictional account of an unsuccessful B-movie actor (played by Jarvis) in 1950s Hollywood who disappeared before completing any major films. The music video is the film-that-could-have-been, patched together from outtakes and unfinished scenes. As well as paying homage to film directors Douglas Sirk and Busby Berkeley, the video draws inspiration from a book of Hollywood star portraits from the 1940s to 1960s created in 1983 by Diane Keaton and Marvin Heiferman, *Still Life: Hollywood Tableaux Photographs*. Many of the scenes in the video reproduced specific film stills from the book, substituting members of Pulp for the original actors.

What a hell of a show...

THE PROMO

Promo of the Month: Pulp – 'This Is Hardcore'
Promo Magazine, March 1998

'This Is Hardcore' is a brilliant recreation of scenes from a lost movie, from a time when the buttoned-up world of the Fifties was about to turn into Sixties freedom and counterculture.

The Technicolor melodrama of Douglas Sirk and imagery of Hitchcock is about to meet *Beat Girl* and *La Dolce Vita*. Scenes are disconnected, include screen tests, and have a virtually surreal relationship to each other.

It's also a much-anticipated video, because of the size of the production; it took nearly five days to shoot at Pinewood. But because of the excellent preparation and timescale of the production, Nichol describes it as one of the most fun promos he's ever done. Partizan executive producer Pete Chambers says the whole crew seemed to be uplifted by the event and pulled out the stops. 'It was a great experience,' he says. 'And it was definitely something about working at Pinewood that made people work that bit harder.'

Nichol agrees that there is certainly a feel of the English Hollywood about this Hollywood pastiche. 'There's a bit of *Peeping Tom* in there,' he says, 'If we'd shot it in Hollywood we would not have got the same feeling at all.' However, the enjoyment comes from the craftsmanship that goes into each shot, from the wonderful casting to the wardrobe styling by Sammy Howarth-Sheldon – she searched and found genuine Fifties clothes that have been hardly used – to the superb art direction by Mark Tanner. Nichol singles out the contribution by Tanner, who recreates that late Fifties Hollywood Technicolor period immaculately through fourteen sets, each colour-coded in the striking primaries of the period.

Nichol says this was the key to getting the Technicolor feel that several other promo directors have also tried to replicate. 'That's the toughest thing,' he says. 'Most people use different stocks or processes, but actually it's nothing to do with that. It's about the costumes, the art direction and hard, direct lighting.'

Nichol brought lighting cameraman Joe Zizzo over from America to shoot it, who did his research, watching Douglas Sirk movies, and ended up using normal film stock. Island commissioner Emma Davis reveals that Jarvis Cocker and Steve Mackey, filmmakers in their own right and closely interested in the video process, have wanted to collaborate with another leading American director, 'for both this one and "Help the Aged", I had to force them to look at scripts.'

Best then not to seek out a story too much. This is a promo about a movie in search of a narrative. After six minutes or so, it does become more focused, as Jarvis drifts off (having been shot) into the Busby Berkeley-type fantasy in which he performs the climax of this epic song. It becomes clear that it's all about betrayal. 'It's a fake world and everyone is smiling,' says Nichol, 'but there's a very dark undercurrent.' Very Pulp, in fact.

YOU ARE

H   C
HA   CO
HAR   COR
HARDCORE
ARD   ORE
RD   RE
D   E

'Hardcore porn takes that wrapping away, and reduces something that is actually quite emotional to a mechanical process. It's too much information. They pick angles that you wouldn't be able to see if you were making love to somebody. Things you shouldn't really see. So it seemed a reasonable metaphor for success. You dream about what being a pop star will be like and, like most things, when you get it, it isn't how you imagined.'
Jarvis Cocker for *Time Out*, 1998

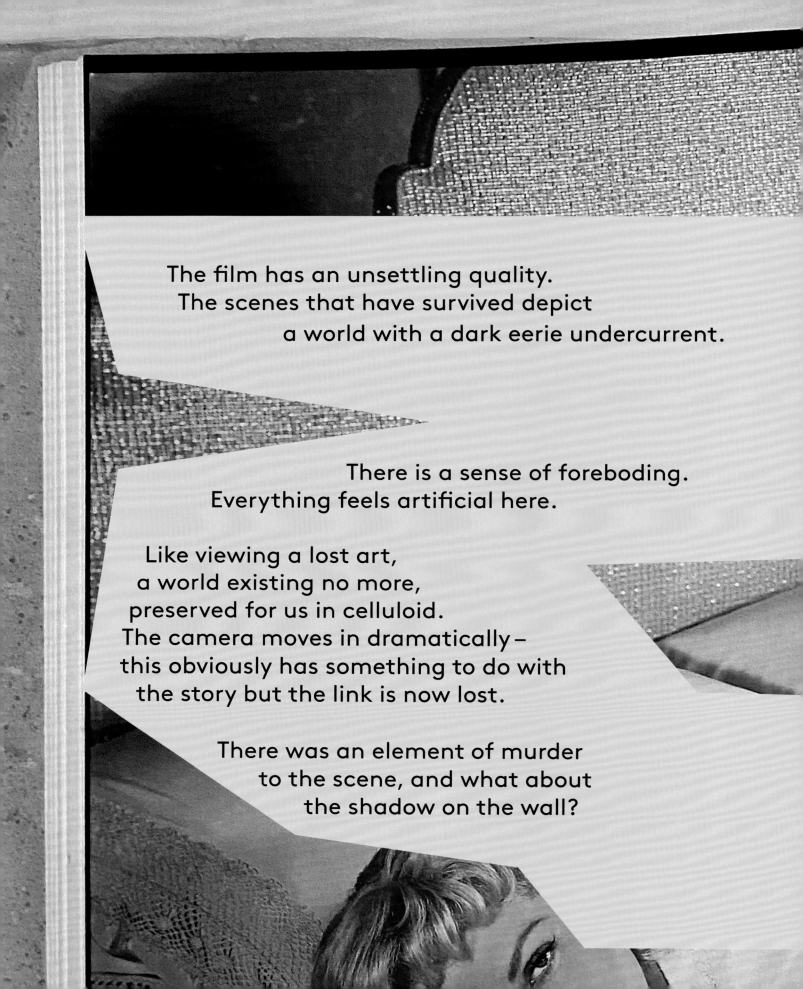

The film has an unsettling quality.
The scenes that have survived depict
a world with a dark eerie undercurrent.

There is a sense of foreboding.
Everything feels artificial here.

Like viewing a lost art,
a world existing no more,
preserved for us in celluloid.
The camera moves in dramatically –
this obviously has something to do with
the story but the link is now lost.

There was an element of murder
to the scene, and what about
the shadow on the wall?

An unapologetic
incandescent
light turned
on at the
party's
end.

Like polyester
dreaming of shot silk.
Find the beauty it's growing up through
the street, right up through the
concrete.

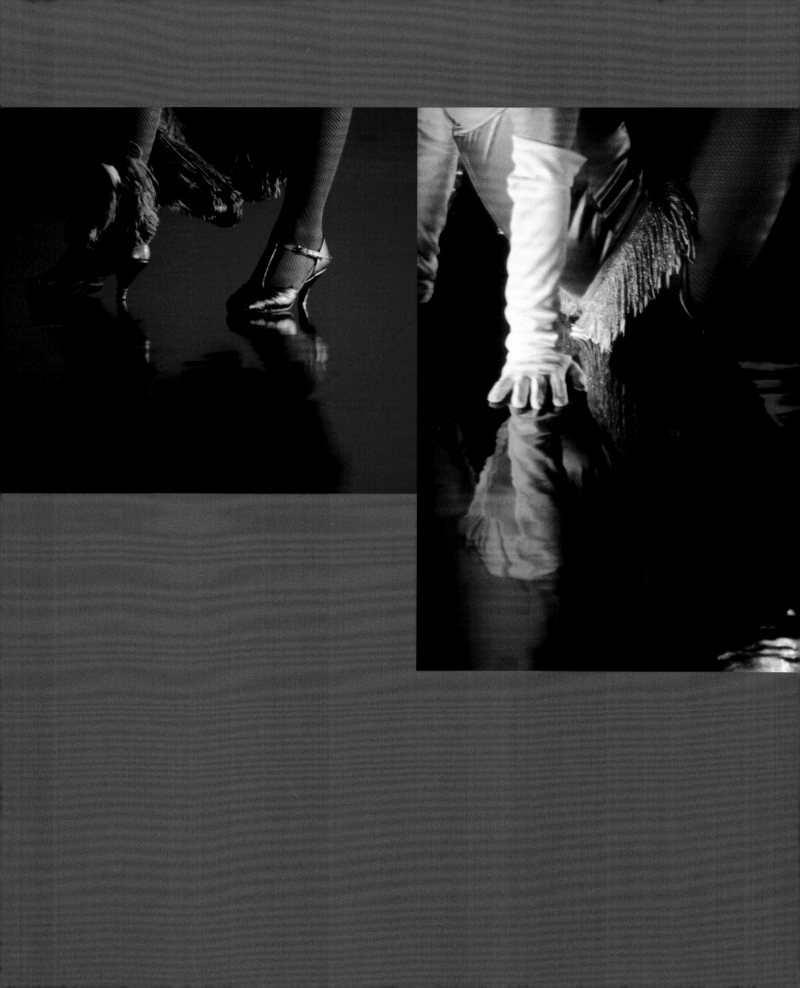

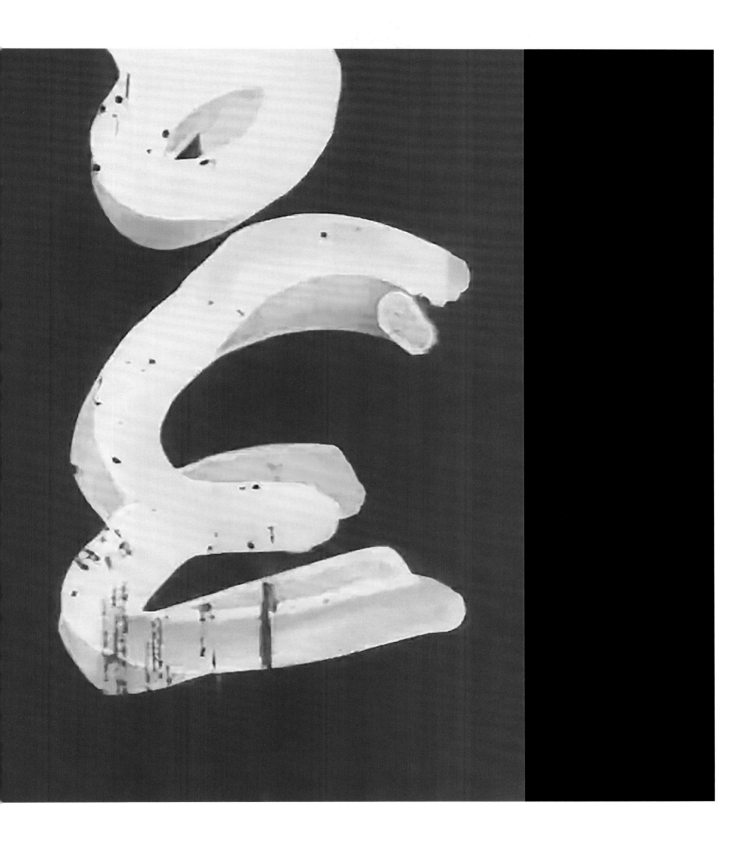

PROD.
"HARDCORE"
DIRECTOR
LEWIS FULTON
CAMERAMAN
HARRY SURTESS
SLATE
TAKE
2

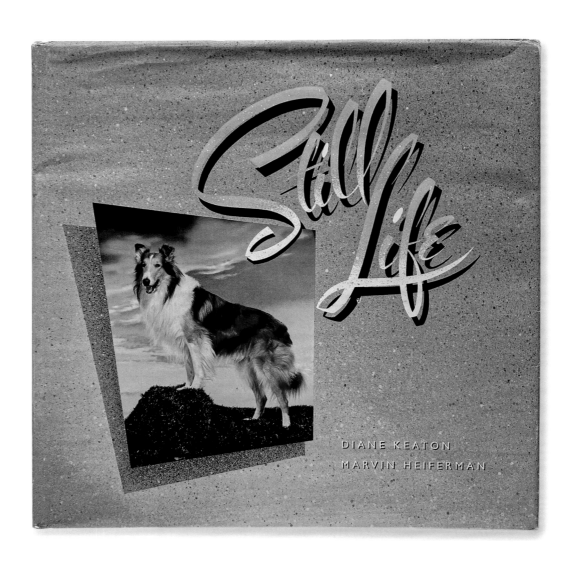

STILL LIFE

Doug Nichol

That summer I was in a used book shop in lower Manhattan and I found a book called *Still Life*, by Diane Keaton and Marvin Heiferman. It was a collection of promotional photos taken on Hollywood film sets by anonymous photographers in the 1950s and 60s. I brought it back to London and stuck it on a bookshelf with a bunch of other art and photo books – and, for a while, I forgot about it.

When I got sent Pulp's 'This Is Hardcore' track, I couldn't believe what a beautiful piece of music it was. The lyrics, about fantasy and role-playing, felt like a movie. I picked up the *Still Life* book and there was something about those images and the music together that sparked an idea.

I wrote up something that was less a music-video treatment and more one of those *Time Out* reviews you'd read about an obscure film opening at the Curzon cinema that week. The idea was that a group of film archivists had found a bunch of film reels from an incomplete movie, titled *This Is Hardcore*, that was made for Embassy Pictures in 1957. The director, Lewis Fulton, had been fired mid-way through production and the studio pulled the plug on his movie. The archivists had restored the film as best they could without a script, piecing together the scenes, the screen tests and whatever else they could find to try to understand what the film was about.

Jarvis and Steve liked the idea and they had recently watched Douglas Sirk's *Written on the Wind* (1956), so we were all coming from the same place on this and excited to make it together. We filmed it at Pinewood Studios on two soundstages right next to where, at the time, Stanley Kubrick was shooting *Eyes Wide Shut*. We had the *Still Life* book on set as reference for many of the film's scenes. I think everyone who worked on the project felt really inspired not only by the song itself, but also by the challenge of trying to pull off something of this scale and capture the feeling of that Technicolor era of the 1950s.

P U L P
"This Is Hardcore"

Partizan/Midi Minuit
10 December 1997
Doug Nichol

This is a film that was made in Technicolor in 1957 by Embassy Pictures, but never shown. All that is left are the outtakes, the wardrobe and screen tests and some scenes deemed too "avant-garde" for the studio at the time. It was made near the end of Hollywood's golden era, and the scenes that have survived depict a world full of sunny smiles and happy people, yet with a dark, eerie undercurrent that may have been the reason the film was never completed.

The star of this film was a young, charismatic singer named Troy Tulane (we see that from the name on the Embassy Pictures slate on the wardrobe tests). A good looking kid with glasses, he was making his debut here. From his various scenes you can see someone who had real promise - his singing, moodiness, even his dancing had a kind of raw, captivating power. After the failure of this film he disappeared and not much is known of him since, but what is left here stands as a testament to his talent.

But the scenes that remain of this film are fascinating. Linked together by bits of screen and wardrobe tests and the one surviving musical number that remains, the film has an unsettling quality. The rescued song, "This Is Hardcore", was well ahead of it's time. You can see how nearly a decade later composers such as John Barry and others were influenced by it in their work.

It's not quite clear if it was a drama or a musical, but the filmmakers were breaking new ground here. The lighting and camera work make use of the studio style "look" of the era with rich colors and distinctive movement, but there is a strange kind of "darkness" which permeates the set, a dark kind of foreboding which has a powerful effect with the music and the images where all the actors are trying their best to show this happy, beautiful world, but end up in a way looking like stuffed animals in a beautiful diorama at the Museum of Natural History.

Everything feels artificial here. The scenes of Troy driving with the rear-projection of the city streets behind him. The young blonde next to him. Where were they going? Does it matter? The scene that comes after it is missing so we'll never know. Another scene involves some actors in a company's boardroom going over the designs for the "Cars of the Future". The gray-haired CEO is pointing out some specific detail, but what is the man in the background trying to conceal in his coat pocket? It's all very dramatic, but we'll never know the answer.

Another section of the film has a beautiful red head waiting in white satin sheets for someone to arrive. And then there is that girl trying in vain to bite the red candied apple that swings on a string in front of her. The director used prism lenses to create an effect with swirling orange pumpkins around her head. These and other images have a look which greatly affected the director Michael Powell who obviously copied much of the filmic style for his movie "Peeping Tom" three years later.

One of my favorite scenes is the segments surrounding the musical number. We see some actors at the beach (a fake beach with painted sky and ocean and rocks). They do take after take as they walk towards us in slow motion, their beaming smiles and laughter creating a haunting mood with the music. Troy Tulane has one of his best moments in a choreographed musical number that tips it's hat to Busby Berkley a bit. Two dozen dancers make their way up and down a huge staircase in formal evening wear, their movements and dancing are fantastic going against the beat of the music. The camera moves with Troy as he enters and sings, moving up the huge staircase with the dancers - it's one of those moments that would have made cinematic history had the film been released, but at least now in it's restored version we can see it in all it's glory.

The sets, art direction, wardrobes, and make-up are absolutely fantastic. Seeing them now, is like viewing a kind of lost art, a

world existing no more and yet preserved for us on celluloid. The wardrobe and make-up tests are very interesting interspersed here between the film's scenes. We can see the actors, bits of the film's crew and the edges of the sets. The white chalked slate reading "Embassy Pictures - "Hardcore" - 2/8/57 - Scene 32b - Bedroom Scene". The wardrobe girl adjusting Troy's hat just right. Maybe a bit of his real persona coming through, but when the camera rolls, he ices over and is back in character. We see the other actors as well and their fascinating names. "Angie Cassell", "Dub Taylor", "Biff Avery", "Nick Peters", "Connie Martin" and so on. Incredible faces.

There is another scene in a beauty parlor with a woman being manicured, pedicured, eyes taped up, mud on the face - being attended to by several beauticians. The beauty treatments are amazing and at the same time we see someone stealing diamonds from her purse. The camera moves in dramatically. This obviously had something to do with the story, but the link is now lost.

From what I can piece together there was an element of murder to the film. Several scenes feature a policeman who seems to be searching for someone. Is the murderer Troy Tulane? Without the other scenes, it's difficult to ascertain. But there is that fantastic push in on the face of the brunette as she turns and SCREAMS silently into the camera (the original sound has been lost) and then later that shot of Tulane and the dead couple in bed. And what about the shadow on the wall? Everything seems to point to him, but without the rest we'll never know.

The people making this film were really onto something and it's in their honor that what is left of this film has been assembled here. After the studio pulled the plug, most of them drifted into relative obscurity - Lewis Fulton, the director, never fully recovered and died a broken man some years later of an overdose in a seedy Berlin hotel.

It's as an homage to them that we show this film now.

"This Is Hardcore" opens in late January.

* * * * *

PULP "THIS IS HARDCORE"
SCENES
13 JANUARY 1998

MAJOR SETS

1. BUSBY BERKLEY MUSICAL DANCE NUMBER SET

Set: Big Curtains, Spotlights, Shinny black lino floor, Color Smoke EFX, Large turntable for dancers/top shots.

Cast: 20 Female Dancers

WD: "Chorus Line" style top hats and tails or with large feather fans.

2. REAR-SCREEN PROJECTION/DRIVING SET

Set: Rear-projection screen, classic convertible car, rain EFX.

Projection Elements: USA countdown leader
Various "picture starts here", etc
Rear View NYC night driving
Side View NYC night driving
Rear View NYC day driving
Side View NYC day driving

Cast: 1 Girl (Early 20s - same as Bedroom Scene?)

Scenes: Rear-Screen driving in Car
Various performance
Projection CU's
Front Projection on face/body

3. HOTEL BEDROOM SET

Set: Bedroom with great bed and padded headboard. Mirror and dressing table - large area. "Written On The Wind" Girl Dancing with herself - waiting for her man. Love Scene/Kiss

Cast: 1 Sexy Girl (Early 20's)
1 Bad Guy

4. OFFICE SET

Set: Classic "Sam Spade" type office - venetian blinds, door with frosted glass windows "Private Detective", overhead lamps OR "Written On The Wind" style office with large oil painting. Desk with gun in drawer. Urgent Telegrams.

Jarvis tied to chair under lamp - playback "Dial M For Murder" Telephone scene with girl

Cast: 2 Toughguys with Tommy Guns (with light EFX) - (same as stuntmen)
1 Girl

5. LIVINGROOM/DINING ROOM/BAR SET

Cast: Family (Father, Mother, Son, Daughter, 2 Grandparents?)
Party (8 people in Fancy Dress) Black Butler/Maid
2 Stuntmen

Scenes: Norman Rockwell Family Dinner -
Drunk at Bar/throw drink at mirror
Cocktail Party - Dancing

Fight Scene (2 Stuntmen) - Big Punch out/Glass Break

6. EXT. SIDEWALK/STREET SET

Cast: 2 Policemen
20 Crowd Extras
1 Dead Man

Scene: Dead Man on curb with on-lookers and police.

Set: Street with curb and 2 cars, storefront window, distant city background, etc.

We were to utilize two sound stages at Pinewood studios, which set the mood for an exciting few weeks of designing, building and dressing a total of around fourteen sets. We didn't have an enormous budget, but the producers were savvy enough to realize that the work of the art department had to be a priority.

Doug and I sat down and went through the research he and I had gathered. We swapped images from the tons of books we had foraged – the internet being but a nascent dream back then. A few days later, I came back with sketches of the bigger sets and various boards and images that would inform the design of the project.

The sets were built and the prop houses trawled for the furniture and décor the period demanded. Joe Zizzo, the director of photography, then spun his magic and recreated the film lighting of that era perfectly.

Art Director, Mark Tanner, 2023

THIS IS HARDCORE

Jarvis wants to make a half hour programme which explores some of the themes contained in the songs on the new album.

To get ball rolling, he wants to involve the cast, crew and sets of the music video.

There is therefore a documentary crew on Pinewood from Tuesday to Thursday shooting some of the strange and wondrous sights the making of a video throws up.

They will also be looking to interview both cast and crew for personal opinions on all matters

from heaven to hardcore.

Ya Mo Be There.

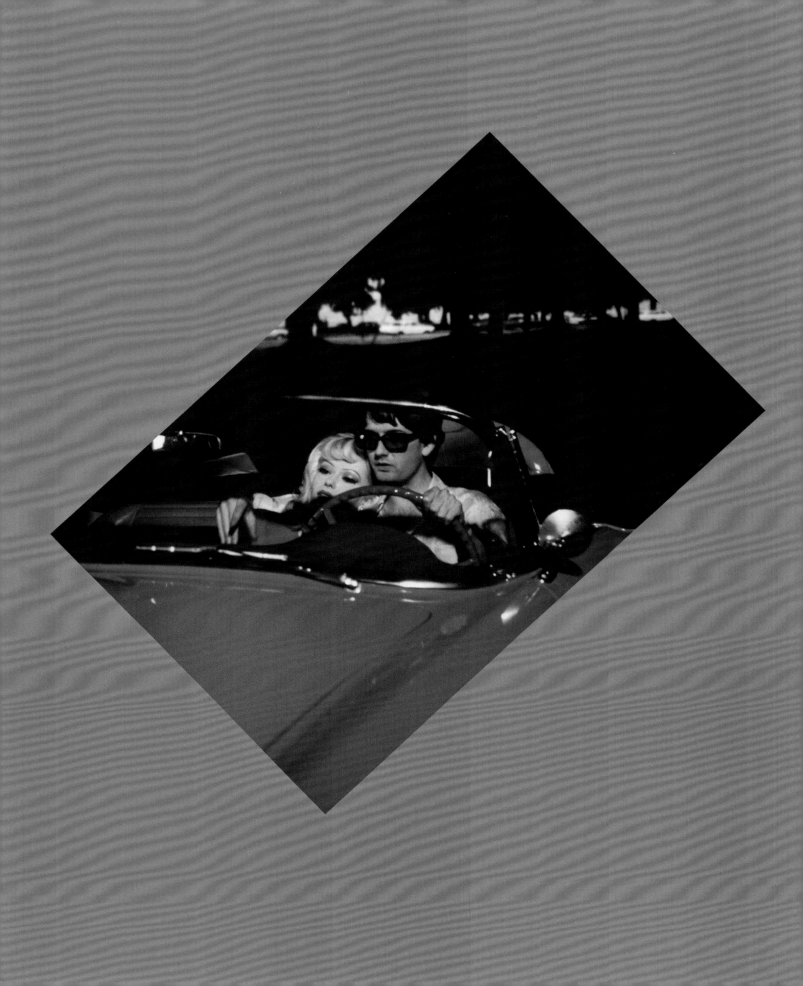

Opposite:
Opening II (1994), John Stezaker.
Collage 24 cm x 16.8 cm.

Next page:
Untitled (1985), John Stezaker.
Silkscreen on canvas 145 x 290 cm.
Courtesy of The Approach gallery.

STOP, WATCH AND THINK

Sergei Sviatchenko
Excerpts from a conversation with Louise Colbourne

Sergei Sviatchenko was born and grew up in Ukraine where he studied architecture and was a representative of the 'Ukrainian New Wave' in the 1980s. He has since become one of the most influential collage artists of our time. Sergei's work has evolved in response to the broad spectrum of cultural shifts and political events that have surrounded his life. He now lives and works in Viborg, Denmark and I met with him at his Less *studio to talk about his life as an artist, the processes he employs to motivate his prolific practice and what the* This Is Hardcore *album meant for him.*

I have built my own 'universe' which operates according to the satisfaction of my personal rules and theories. The goals and objectives that I set in myself, in my collage practice, represent endless freedom in choosing topics, combinations of elements and colour relationships, which give me the opportunity to say that the maximum result is achieved only when the thought is absolutely absurd and free, and the technique is perfect. I construct my images-verses intuitively, based on the 'archive of memory', building this or that plot with the help of scissors and glue – trying to create a balance known only to me.

This kind of careful work is very similar to how a person builds his own path – carefully and intuitively moving forward, making important steps or making mistakes. The collage, in my opinion, fully reflects the fragmentation of our life; hurried, superficial and full of the desire to stop, watch and think. Collage, like life, can sometimes be satisfying, creative, and sometimes disturbing and provocative. I don't know how I would continue to enjoy life if I did not make this work.

This Is Hardcore was a soundtrack of our very happy years as a young family with three kids, who are grownups now with kids of their own. The content was probably too sophisticated for them back then, but the richness of the music and cinematographic atmosphere made us happy to listen to the album countless times...

And now the time has come to use Paul's photographs to make a new reality.

Opposite and the following three pages:
Less (2022), Sergei Sviatchenko.
Digital collage series, size variable.

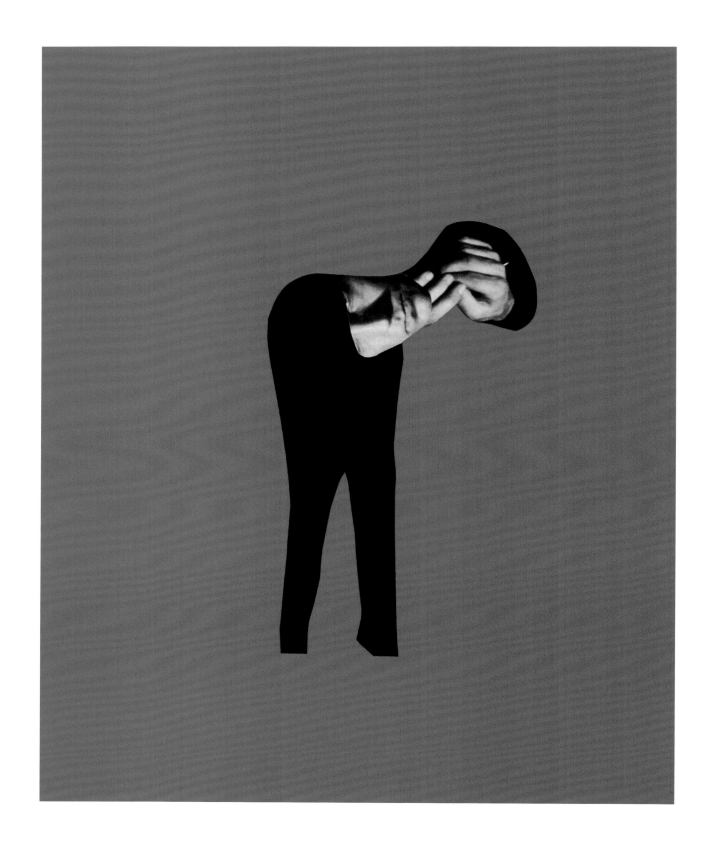

HELP THE AGED

Director: Hammer & Tongs/Garth Jennings
Art Director: John Currin
Produced by: Nick Goldsmith
Shoot Date: 17–18 October 1997
Locations: Stoke Newington Town Hall ('stair lift and old people's
home' scenes) and White City Studio, Silver Road, London
(green screen 'space' scenes)

Released on the 11th November 1997, 'Help the Aged' was the first single released from *This Is Hardcore*. It reached number eight in the charts and the video was voted International Video of the Year 1998 by The Music Video Production Association. This is the only Pulp music video where Jarvis is wearing glasses – shades with a brown tint. The atmosphere takes influence from the 1946 Powell and Pressburger film, *A Matter of Life and Death*.

The first part of the video, filmed in Stoke Newington Town Hall, displays the kind of hues and colourways one might associate with the 1970s. Paintings by John Currin hang on the olive-green walls, their characters staring out into the lens, while Jarvis – in a brown suit and doused in orange light – rises on a super-long Stannah stairlift mouthing the words with slight tilts of the head. At the top of the stairs Jarvis exits the stairlift with an ironically energetic leap to join the rest of Pulp playing their instruments in a room furnished with stylish furniture and soft light from domestic table lamps. In between takes, members of the band play with 'clackers' in the dressing room.

Candida, wearing a red cardigan, moves her hands across keys that are tilted 45 degrees away from her while other characters begin to emerge, a woman crawls across a ping-pong table, while another sips from the type of water fountain you might find in a school hallway. By this point, the young men in the video have grown grey bushy beards and hair, yet the women remain young and sexy – perhaps a telling reflection of societal acceptance of ageing between the genders.

Reality rapidly slips away, as the video shoot moves from the greens of the Town Hall to the green-screen set at White City Studio. Suddenly there are many stairlifts, shooting their passengers off the face of the earth – looking like multiple cocktail sticks in one massacred cube of cheese at a party buffet. The band continues to play but, this time, on a platform rising higher and higher in an expansive sci-fi kingdom – which is later revealed to be at the centre of a supernova. Bang.

Following page:
John Currin, *The Neverending Story*, 1994.
Ink on paper, 53.0 x 45.2 x 3.8 cm.
Courtesy of Sadie Coles Gallery.

THE PAINTINGS AND THE PAINTED

Excerpts from memoirs by Pat and Jo Skinny

The 'Help the Aged' video featured reproductions of John Currin's paintings, hanging on the walls of Stoke Newington Town Hall. The scenes were constructed to represent an idealized notion of a care home. Currin's painting The Neverending Story *also appeared on the cover of the single 'Help the Aged'. The paintings are darkly humorous, exploring the genre of portraiture by critiquing gender stereotypes and the male gaze. Jarvis was struck by Currin's images of older powerful men surrounded by women who seem to be sucking up to them, but really they are thinking: 'What a jerk!'. There was a connection made between these paintings and themes of the album* This Is Hardcore.

The director Garth Jennings and Jarvis Cocker thought it would be a neat bookend to the 'Disco 2000' video to feature us in the 'Help the Aged' video as the retired and aged couple from the 'Disco 2000' video behaving badly in their dotage.

We were due to fly to New York on the same evening as the make-up and costume design test-call day for 'Help the Aged'. Jo and I were the obvious people to use as guinea pigs because, as the stylists, we ran the costume dept and could also feature in the videos.

So, we rock up early (having packed for New York the night before – bags left ready in the hallway of our West End flat for a quick exit after work). The make-up [for the video] is very involved, including prosthetics, ageing applications, wrinkle schnizzle, wigs and beards. The costume is upper class; inherited tweeds, silk scarves, tea dresses, pearls etc., inspired by the John Currin paintings that formed the backbone of the look.

The makeover was hilariously unnerving and dark – perfect. We both had enormous powdered bouffant wigs, draggy make-up on wrinkled skin – think Miss Havisham and Abraham Lincoln through a Ready Steady Go!/Redlands after party fallout lens! I think it was Jarvis who decided, ultimately, that Jo's character looked too cruel and ugly, and the women were scrapped. I apparently, was just ugly enough!

The day ran on and it was getting very close to our flight time, so we called a cab, changed into our street clothes and headed home in full make-up – which we planned to scrape off back at the flat. On our arrival, we realized, to our dread, that we had locked ourselves out. No Google on smart phones, no idea what to do. In full-on Abe Lincoln make-up and a vintage adidas tracksuit I went door-to-door (including the local fire station) asking people for a locksmith. We eventually got one out and managed to dive in, grab our suitcases and passports, and go straight to the airport – still in full make-up (and tracksuits). We had fifteen minutes in a Heathrow Airport toilet to pull off wigs and prosthetics and present our weird faces at the check in. No one batted an eyelid (different times!) and we were rushed onto the plane with melting faces – the only time that the Aged Deborah was seen by the public.

IT'S OKAY TO LONG AS AS YOU

MAKING 'PULP: A FILM ABOUT LIFE, DEATH & SUPERMARKETS'

Florian Habicht

In August 2012, I woke up in my Airbnb bed in Williamsburg NYC. I'd had a night on the town after the rooftop screening of my NYC-shot romance film *Love Story*. Before going to sleep, I was high on life and sent an email to the director of the London Film Festival. It was a link to a glowing review of my film in *Variety* – a last attempt to get their attention, as I was giving up hope of the festival selecting my film. I had made an innovative, punky feature film that I was proud of, but getting it selected for festivals was as hard as it's always been for this independent filmmaker from New Zealand.

Anyway... I opened my eyes that morning, reached for my laptop and in my inbox was an email from the London Film Festival. It was an invitation for *Love Story* to screen at the 2012 festival. I couldn't believe it! I was over the moon and my first thought was who could I invite? Not knowing many people in London, I thought about inviting Jarvis Cocker. Queen and Pulp are my favourite bands and, living at the end of the earth in New Zealand, meeting your idols is often just a dream, but here I was presented with an opportunity. I couldn't invite Freddie Mercury, for obvious reasons, and so I drafted an email to Jarvis. I asked my girlfriend Teresa (living in Berlin at the time) to check my message. She thought I was naive and full of wishful thinking but encouraged me to send it, along with a link to the film's trailer. I sent the email off, heard nothing back for weeks and gave up hope.

That October, I was in London for the BFI Film Festival and one wet and cold morning I found myself sitting at a café in Brick Lane. It was a packed, cosy vibe and most people had their heads down in their laptops – sheltering from the weather. I was one of them, working in my remote office, promoting the upcoming screenings of my film. Suddenly an email landed in my inbox from Jarvis's manager Jeannette Lee. They had enjoyed the trailer and Jarvis wanted to attend the *Love Story* screening. Like a football fan whose team had just scored a goal, I jumped up from my seat and shouted 'Woohoo!'. Everyone at the café stopped what they were doing and looked up at me. For a moment I was lost for words, like a possum blinded by headlights. I sat back down in my seat and read the email again. Everyone went back to their business.

The next week, I met Jarvis at the Curzon Cinema café and ordered us cups of tea. While waiting at the counter, I turned my head back and saw the lead singer of Pulp checking his phone. It was a surreal moment for me. We clicked immediately. I think our first conversation was about flat white coffee, which was invented in Wellington, New Zealand. Jarvis told me he needs to drink a cup of tea in the morning before having his coffee. So British, I thought.

Jarvis told me about Parkhill, Sheffield – the largest housing estate project in the whole of Europe. He showed me a photo of the famous graffiti message turned into neon signage: 'Clare Middleton, I love you, will you Marry Me?'. Jarvis told me he wanted to make a film about the lives of people who live at Park Hill, to follow their lives 'without stalking them' and then follow some of them to the upcoming Pulp concert in Sheffield. But he couldn't get the idea funded and gave up on making the film. I was amazed to hear his idea because I had an idea with a very similar sentiment. Mine was to make a film set in a day in the life of Sheffield, where the people of Sheffield are given as much of the spotlight as the band – and then Pulp play their final hometown show that night. Jarvis said it was a pity that there wasn't enough time to organize the making of a film, with the concert being less than two months away. With a glint of hope in my eyes, I replied by saying two months is a long time. Later that week, Jarvis and Jeannette invited me to make the film about Pulp – provided I was able to secure the funding.

My British filmmaker friend Alex Boden, who had studied filmmaking with me in Amsterdam, loved Pulp and agreed to produce the film with me. We pitched our film with the working title 'Common People' to Channel Four Television. We told them that the idea was to focus on the real people of Sheffield as the stars of the film. It was my plan to include re-enactments and fabricated scenes on a film set that really got them excited. I have a feeling this might have inspired the concept of Nick Cave's *20,000 Days on Earth* (2014), which Channel Four was working on at the time. Channel Four disappeared on us and Jarvis was not so keen on the re-enactment, staged, ideas of mine – including him swimming laps in speedos the morning of the concert and the co-author of this book, Paul Burgess, being dressed as a circus clown in an elevator retelling the famous Michael Jackson incident. We decided to keep the film very real. Alex decided to bankroll the epic concert shoot on his credit card and seek funding after the shoot. This was the only way we could shoot the film in the short amount of time that we had!

In December 2012, the middle of winter, I found myself sitting on a train from London, heading to the North of England. Pulp were, meanwhile, touring in hot and sunny South America before their final Sheffield gig. In my hands was Jarvis's lyric book *Mother, Brother, Lover*. Jarvis had given it to me, with certain lyrics underlined and scribbled comments and notes on the songs. Not having done any research on Sheffield, and Pulp's history, this was my roadmap to making the film. I remember one lyric mentioned Castle Market and Jarvis had underlined this and scribbled 'worth a visit' next to it.

With the book and gear, I got off at Sheffield station, hopped into a cab, checked into a self-contained apartment and then walked to the nearby pub. It was already dark at 5pm, freezing cold, everything looked grey and I felt homesick. I was alone and my core crew, of Alex Boden, DOP Maria Ines Manchego, sound recordist Mark Bull and editor Peter O'Donoghue, were arriving a week later from all corners of the globe. The picture I had painted myself of Sheffield from listening to Pulp's songs was colourful, sexy and sunny, but this city reminded me more of Hamilton in New Zealand. I felt like the first trooper dropped in by parachute.

At the pub, the waitress arrived with my fish 'n' chips and her strong Northern accent. The fish was cold. I had a beer to wash it down. I then rushed back to my room, to do a live radio interview with a Melbourne radio station – for the Australian cinema release of *Love Story*. Because of the Pulp shoot, I couldn't be in Australia to promote my NYC film in person. I got on the call and enthusiastically told the Radio DJ how I met people on the streets of NYC, and (on camera) asked them for

Victoria Live at Home Singing Group: Margaret Allen, John Platts, Alan Headford, Valerie Dronfield, Andrea Vintin, Pat Gormanby, Mo Baxter, Beryl Reaney, Janet Maillard and Lorna Marshall.

Location: Roof Top Cafe, Castle Market, Sheffield.

This and previous page: Stills taken from *Pulp: A Film About Life, Death & Supermarkets* (2014) directed by Florian Habicht.

ideas for the film, and then acted them out with Ukrainian-born, Russian actress Masha Yakovenko. I told the people of Melbourne how my film and our love affair was dictated by the spontaneous and wild ideas of real New Yorkers. The DJ asked me another question and, thinking I was going to release a fart, I ended up releasing more. Diarrhoea to be precise. My first Sheffield meal did not agree with me! I continued raving enthusiastically about filming in NYC while taking off my pants and wiping my legs clean. The DJ, and Australian listeners, had no idea of what was happening to me in Sheffield. That's show-business.

Two years later, when *Pulp: A Film about Life, Death & Supermarkets* screened at the majestic Ace Hotel Theatre in Los Angeles, I told the diarrhoea story to the audience and Jarvis, who was next to me on the stage, couldn't believe what he was hearing. He had a cheeky grin on his face. Before our film began that night, he warmed up the crowd by saying common phrases in a thick Sheffield accent and then translating them into more formal British for the American audience. It was hilarious. Suddenly I felt like we were doing a stand-up routine. Tiffany Anders, who organized the Don't Knock the Rock screening, asked the packed theatre who had seen my films before? One single person shouted out from the crowd. Jarvis responded to me: 'Your mum's in the audience!'

Beck and his band were in the crowd and, months later, asked me if I'd like to make a concert film with them. It didn't eventuate, but people loved the film that night. One of the scenes that got the most applause was the elderly diners and their moving rendition of 'Help the Aged'. I will never forget filming that scene.

Alex had contacted Sheffield's Victoria Live at Home Singing Group and I emailed them the lyrics to Pulp's 'Help the Aged'. We had obtained permission to film at Castle Market, at a café that was very popular with the oldie regulars. I really wanted regular Sheffield people to sing Pulp's songs in the film, and we had already shot the Sheffield Harmony Choir singing 'Common People'. So the film would be a musical.

When we arrived at the Roof Top café, Castle Market on the morning of filming, the owner's first words were that we only had one hour to shoot our scene. Expecting we had at least half the day up our sleeve, this was a shock. Then our singing group arrived early, before we had set up. They had brought a guitarist, which was a pleasant surprise. He had rehearsed the song with them. I asked the group how they felt about singing a song about ageing and they felt it was poignant. I asked if they had learned the lyrics and not a single person had memorized them. My heart dropped. We only had an hour to set up and shoot. Each singer was holding a crinkled printed sheet of the song lyrics. I was quick on my feet and thought we could hide the lyrics inside newspapers. In filmmaker survival mode, I ran downstairs to a magazine shop at the market and found a bundle of old magazines that contained tabloid headlines like 'Murder!' and 'She stole my wife!' – perfect for hiding lyric sheets behind. We shot the scene with two cameras and captured it in three takes. Leaving things up to chance and rocking and rolling in the moment is something I love the most about filmmaking. But it almost bit us in the foot this time. These classic magazines and the raw energy worked in our favour. The Victoria Live at Home Singing Group were magic, and their performance is one of my favourite scenes in the film. The band also loved it.

The scariest moment of making the film was me travelling to my first interview at Jarvis's house. We had decided that I would shoot the interview myself with no DOP, no sound person and no crew – so the interview could be as intimate as possible. Anyway, Alex helped me get into a taxi with all the gear and I took off. The fierce looking taxi driver started having an intense argument on the phone, with lots of 'f' and 'c' words, and five minutes into the journey I realized I hadn't given him an address yet. I went to tell him the address, he told me to shut the fuck up and continued his argument. I almost pooped my pants again and ended up having an absurd text exchange with Alex. When I finally gave the driver the address, and arrived, Jarvis cheered me up immediately.

I think we made a special film. I was proud of Candida for being brave and sharing some tough things for the first time in front of the camera. Meeting young Liberty on Stanhope Road and hearing her thoughts on growing up too fast really moved me – she is now a young mother! Ordering a kiddie lunch box set (each) on a filming break with Jarvis was another highlight. We each had a mini sandwich, a mini hot chocolate and a toy. Living life when life is worth living. My only regrets are not managing to include my favourite Pulp song 'Dishes' in the final edit and forgetting to ask Jarvis if he sings in the shower.

Jarvis Cocker and Florian Habicht.
Photograph by: Dana Distortion.

Stoke Newington Town Hall, art deco staircase, White City, Hammer & Tongs, Stannah stairlift, John Currin's paintings, The Neverending Story, Matters of Life and Death, stairway to heaven, Powell and Pressburger, Operation Ethel, green screen, table tennis, playing with 'clackers' in the dressing room, bushy false beards, transmission, help the undead.

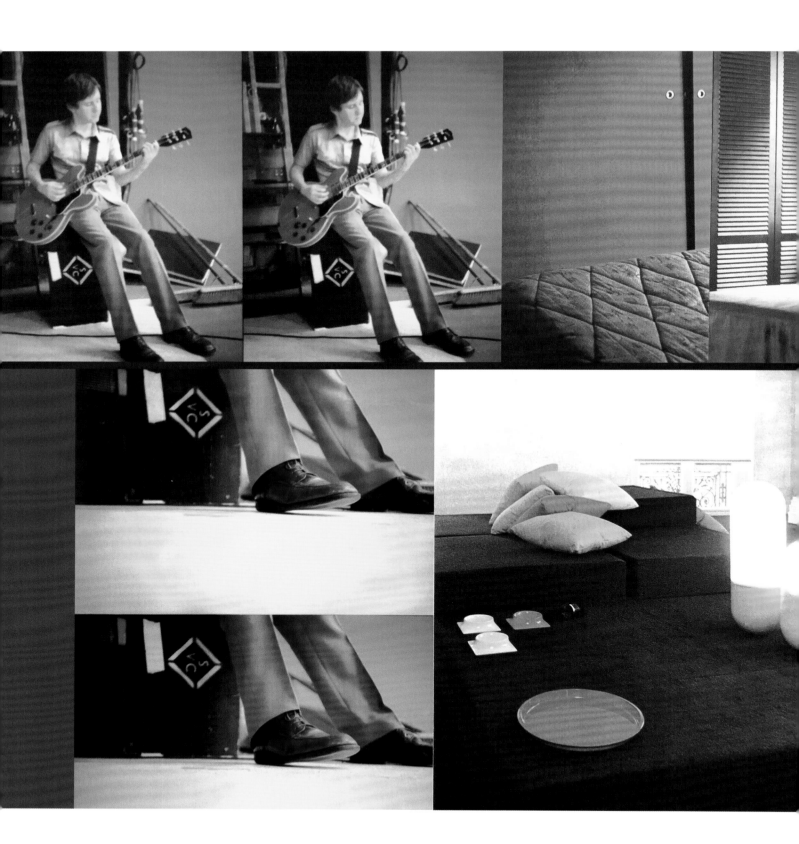

'The song was born out of a very real fear of dying. Everybody knows they're going to die eventually and nobody likes it – or the thought of getting older and not being able to do what you used to do. Because we live in such a youth-oriented society, I think people are actually more scared of not being young anymore than the thought of getting old. They don't perceive very much that's attractive about adulthood, so they extend their adolescence to ridiculous lengths, myself included.

'I guess when I first came up with the line I found it a bit funny, but often my way of trying to deal with things I'm worried about is to turn them into a song, and hide, instead of confront them.

'Doing that hopefully helps me get through. I've always been aware of ageing, because success did come quite late to us and it's difficult to hold onto your dignity in the pop-music business. If you're older, it gets harder. You're reminded of your age a lot more than other people, because you're always having to look at photo sessions of yourself and think, Jesus, I look fucking rough in that.'

Jarvis Cocker, circa 1998

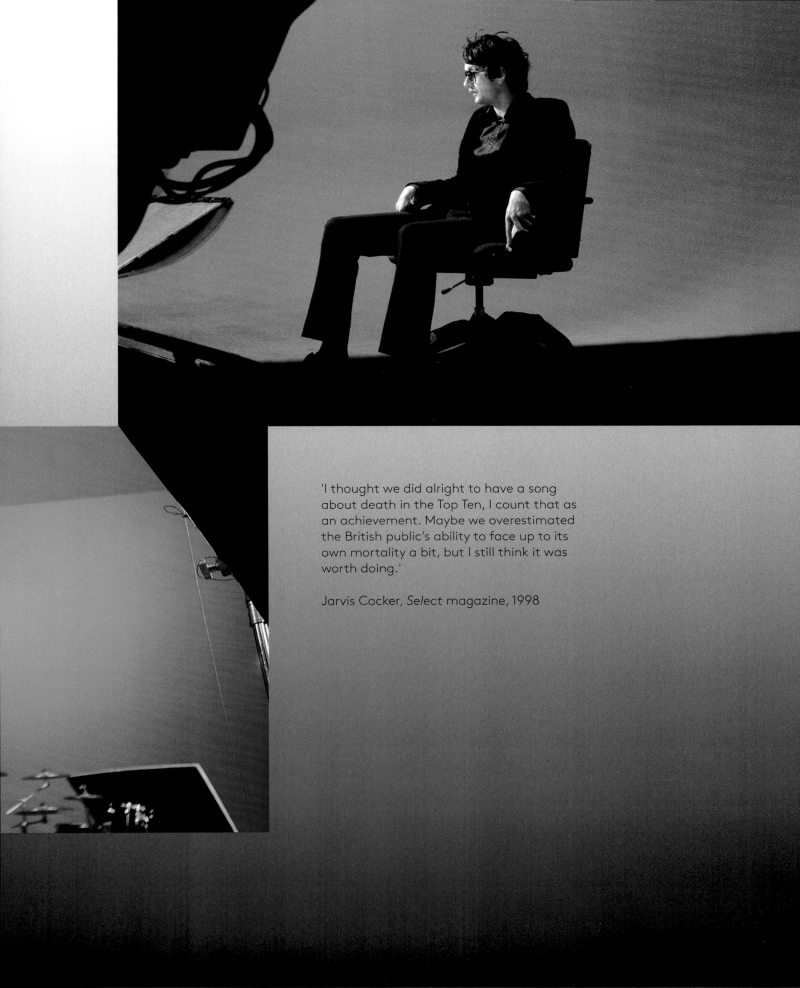

'I thought we did alright to have a song about death in the Top Ten, I count that as an achievement. Maybe we overestimated the British public's ability to face up to its own mortality a bit, but I still think it was worth doing.'

Jarvis Cocker, *Select* magazine, 1998

GARTH JENNINGS IN CONVERSATION WITH JARVIS COCKER, PART ONE

Extract from The Hammer & Tongs Collection DVD, released in 2010.
Garth Jennings (GJ) and Jarvis Cocker (JC)

GJ   Well it was ages ago and ['Help the Aged'] was one of the first videos. It was a bit of a breakthrough for us because it was the first time someone like yourself had really trusted us. So, I wondered why you went with our idea.

JC   Well, we're going back into the mists of time, aren't we? I think it was probably the Stannah stairlift really, that did it. I just thought that was a nice idea for me to be singing on an old person's chairlift. And then the idea of going to heaven via that [chairlift], which kind of referenced the Michael Powell film, *A Matter of Life and Death*. I think that was it. But I've always loved Powell and [Emeric] Pressburger films and I just thought that the first image of me travelling on a stair lift was funny.

GJ   I always liked the idea of a stairlift to heaven and I was so thrilled when you went with it. But also, there were lots of things that then, after we pitched the idea, you had lots of other things that you suggested for us to look at. For example, there were lots of paintings in the video by John Currin.

JC   Who's now one of the most rated artists in the world. I'd seen his work and we knew that we wanted to work with him on the sleeve for *This Is Hardcore*. It was something that chimed to me about his pictures, which seemed to feature old men, with beards, with young women. Maybe I was feeling old already, even though I'm much older now. I remember we had some discussions because I thought they shouldn't really be old people; they should be young blokes made up to look old. Oh, I don't know, there were certain ideas going on and I think you were very patient to facilitate some of those ideas.

GJ   I mean, it was quite an odd video to make as well, and you have always been so hands-on I suppose, as you have always had good ideas of your own. Did you at any point think oh no, this is going terribly wrong?

JC   No, not at all. I think that's when you get the best things, videos that have worked best in the past when you've got ideas of your own and then you add them to somebody else's and then you get something that you couldn't imagine happening. I did wonder how you were going to do heaven, on not the most massive budget in the world. But I think we managed to make a virtue out of the slightly homemade aspect of the scene, which I've always liked anyway. I was very pleased. This is before CGI really took off, but it was already starting to come in a bit, and I've always really felt I liked a bit of a model.

Above:
Image render by Walter Burgess, aged 12 (2022).

The 'heaven' scene in Pulp's 'Help the Aged' video is based on the 'other world' scene from Michael Powell and Emeric Pressburger's film *A Matter of Life and Death* (1946). The scene was inspired by Walsall Bus Station built by AHMM in 1937. The images on these pages are stills from the film displaying the imaginative and ambitious scale of the joint writer-producer-directors of this classic film. The actor David Niven plays a British airman who survives a plane crash and falls in love with an American radio operator played by Kim Hunter. After his parachute fails the airman is summoned to the afterlife, which is portrayed as being situated in a vast modernist-minimalist series of set designs. The cinematographer was Jack Cardiff and the huge sets of the 'other world' scenes were designed by the esteemed production designer Alfred Junge.

The following pages 124–125 contain a digital render by Elfyn Round who has recently graduated with a degree in Film and Television Design from Nottingham Trent University, where he wrote his thesis on the film *A Matter of Life and Death*. In his thesis he discusses the ground-breaking techniques used to make the film at that time, especially for a British studio, as well as the film's satirical sub-plot on Anglo-American relations at the end of WWII. We asked Elfyn to make a digital image inspired by the models made for the 'Help the Aged' scenes (directed by Garth Jennings) and the original Powell and Pressburger film sets made for the film. Elfyn's artwork features the band placed in situ on the white plinth. The photograph used for the render was taken by Paul Burgess when Pulp were performing on set in front of a green screen during the making of the video in 1997.

A
LITTLE
SOUL

Director: Hammer & Tongs/Garth Jennings
Produced by: Nick Goldsmith
Shoot Date: 23–24 April 1998
Location: Olympic Studios, 117 Church Road, Barnes, London, SW13 9HL

The music video for 'A Little Soul' was filmed in Olympic Studios, a location with a rich creative history and the ghosts of the many iconic musicians who had previously recorded there including Jimi Hendrix, Funkadelic, The Rolling Stones, Buzzcocks and Bowie.

The song itself, released on 8 June 1998 and reaching number 22 in the charts, looks at the relationship between Jarvis and his father. There is a vulnerability in the content of the song that is mirrored in the children who appear in the music video – interacting with the members of Pulp. The child actors each play a miniature version of their adult counterpart, and their role in the narrative is to reawaken and remotivate the adult versions of themselves.

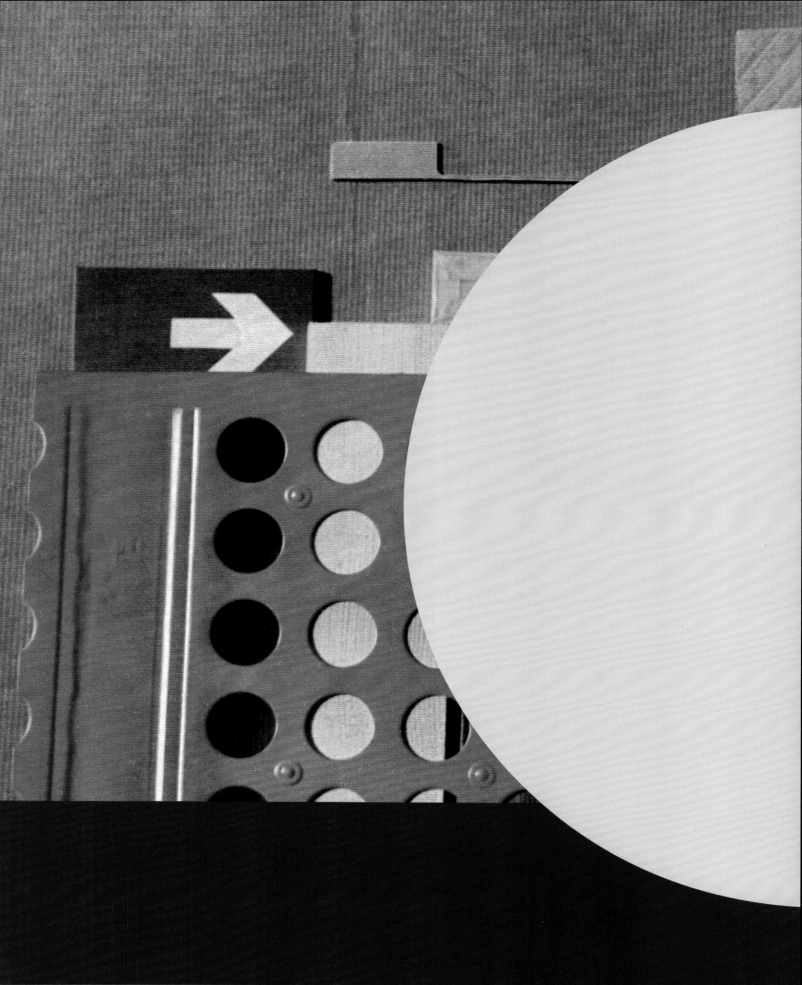

GARTH JENNINGS IN CONVERSATION WITH JARVIS COCKER, PART TWO

Extract from *The Hammer & Tongs Collection* DVD, released in 2010.
Garth Jennings (GJ) and Jarvis Cocker (JC)

GJ   In 'A Little Soul', do you know the little boy who follows you around in the video, the little Jarvis, do you know who he is?

JC   Yeah. I remembered at the time; he is Sophie Ellis-Bextor's brother. I was more excited by the fact that he is the son of Janet Ellis, who used to be on *Jigsaw*, which was one of my favourite programmes as a kid and she was on *Blue Peter* as well, weren't she?

GJ   Yeah, and she turned up with her son [Jackson Ellis Leach, see page 136] for the audition and we just gave him the job straight away. We were so impressed on both levels, mum and son, he was great actually. And, funnily enough, very recently he popped into our office to say hello.

JC   I was thinking about that. I showed the video to my girlfriend the other day and I thought, I wonder what all those kids are doing now?

GJ   Well, he's now a drummer in Sophie's band.

JC   Wow.

GJ   They've all grown up now. Are you pleased with this video for 'A Little Soul' or are there any bits you don't like?

JC   I always thought I should have looked at the camera in the last shot. 'Cause he holds the microphone up and I sing the last couple of lines from the song and I feel that I should have looked at the camera – don't know why. [...] [But], apart from that, I know I was very pleased. I liked, I mean, it was before I had a child, obviously, so it was on my mind and the conceit of the video was like, oh, the kids were like the mini versions of all the members of the band and we were trying to get them together, but the adults were just lazy, horrible, unlikeable people. And I, I quite like that. And I quite like that you don't often see that, do you?

GJ   I was really pleased with it and I also loved the way it turned out looking, it looked really nice and the kids were great.

JC   Maybe it's one of the few examples of a studio-based video – you know, those videos where they have the band playing in the studio – that's actually watchable.

GJ   Yeah, because normally it's horrible. Especially with that one hand on the headphones thing.

JC   Yeah. All that kind of thing.

GJ   We got away with it.

JC   That's always good. You know, those things are always good when you take something that generally is awful and you manage to get away with it. That's always more satisfying.

GJ   But didn't you do a studio video for a 'Bad Cover Version'?

JC   We did, and I think we got away with it again.

GJ   You did it again. You guys! There's no stopping you now.

JC   Yeah, we are the kings of the studio video.

Pulp Shoot.

1. Jarvis & Jack (side room off mixing booth)

a. Jack peeks around doorway
b. Jack silhouetted in doorway
c. Track into Jarvis trashed out on sofa (Jacks POV)
d. Jack looking at Jarvis (mid)
e. Close up - Jack tries to wake Jarvis
f. Jack hands Jarvis mug of tea
g. Jarvis sits up and drinks tea, Jack sits next him (syncs chorus)
h. Jarvis gets up & leaves, jack follows

2. Mark & Jack Shaw (in kitchen)

a. Slow wide (hand held) move towards Mark looking out of window. When near mark looks over his shoulder
b. Cut to opposite angle of Mark front on looking over his shoulder - there is no-one there
c. Behind mark high, jibbing down revealing Jack outside the window through the blinds
d. close up of above

MARK - KITCHEN AREA - BLINDS GO UP SLOWLY...

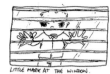
LITTLE MARK AT THE WINDOW.

...REVEAL KID OUTSIDE WINDOW

3. Candida & Ellice (in room below kitchen)

a. Candida curled up on an armchair asleep
b. Close up of Ellice vigorously shaking Candida
c. Candida does not stir
d. portrait of Ellice

CANDIDA ASLEEP IN CONSERVATORY

CANDIDA WON'T WAKE UP.

CHAIR DRAGGED BY GIRL.

4. Steve & Marc in Games room

a. Mid shot of Steve huddled over space invaders machine
b. Mid shot of stve from front playing machine, marc appears out of shadows holding Bass
c. Detail of marc pulling plug on machine
d. Close up uf steve looking evily at Marc
e. Looking down at Marc portrait
f. Marc tries to pull steve away from machine

STEVE ON SPACE INVADERS.

TINY STEVE TUNES THE BASS.

5. Nick & Jackson in main studio

a. Wide shot of Nick sitting in the middle of the studio on a drum stool
b. Closer shot of Nick looking over his shoulder, out of the darkness hurtles Jackson with a cymbal stand raised over his head
c. Close up of Jackson running towards Nick
d. Detail of stand being put on the ground
e. Close up of Nick peering over the top of his paper at Jackson
f. Wide shot of Jackson running around and assembling the kit around Nick
g. Close up of Jackson Lifting up Nicks Foot and sliding the kick drum peddle in.

KID BUILDS DRUM KIT AROUND HIM.

6. All in main studio

a. Looking along piano Candida (still asleep) is pushed up into position
b. Closer track around to side of piano, Ellice arms though Candidas playing piano
c. Steve pulls on guitar lead / Marc picks it up and plugs it back in
d. Nick puts down his paper - reveals rest of band in studio
e. Jarvis in booth mid & close up sync
f. Profile of Jarvis looking out of booth / children come out of darkness
g. Band wide master from behind
h. Looking back to Jarvis wide through Band performance

LIFT UP

TRACK AROUND.

GIRL PLAYS FOR CANDIDA

7. Corridoor

CANDIDA PUSHED DOWN CORRIDOR

KID FOLLOWS MARK MOVING BOX/AMP.

CANDIDA IN LIFT.

8. Mixing booth

TAPE - REEL - DETAILS.

ALL KIDS ON THE DESK.

Opposite page:
Jackson Ellis Leach (aged 35).
Photograph by: Catherine Garcia.

JACKSON ELLIS LEACH

After my career as a child actor, I started playing drums and have been playing professionally as a session drummer for the last sixteen years. I was ten when I played mini-Jarvis in the video for 'A Little Soul'.

I was represented by a children's acting agency, Abacus. I'd been acting for a while, mainly in period dramas, but I hadn't been in any music videos. I met the Hammer & Tongs boys, they were lovely.

I have vivid memories of playing Nick's drum kit on set, it was the first time I had sat behind one. I was usually acting in dramas set in the mid-19th century, so there was never a kit around at work before that! I'm sure it had an influence on my future.

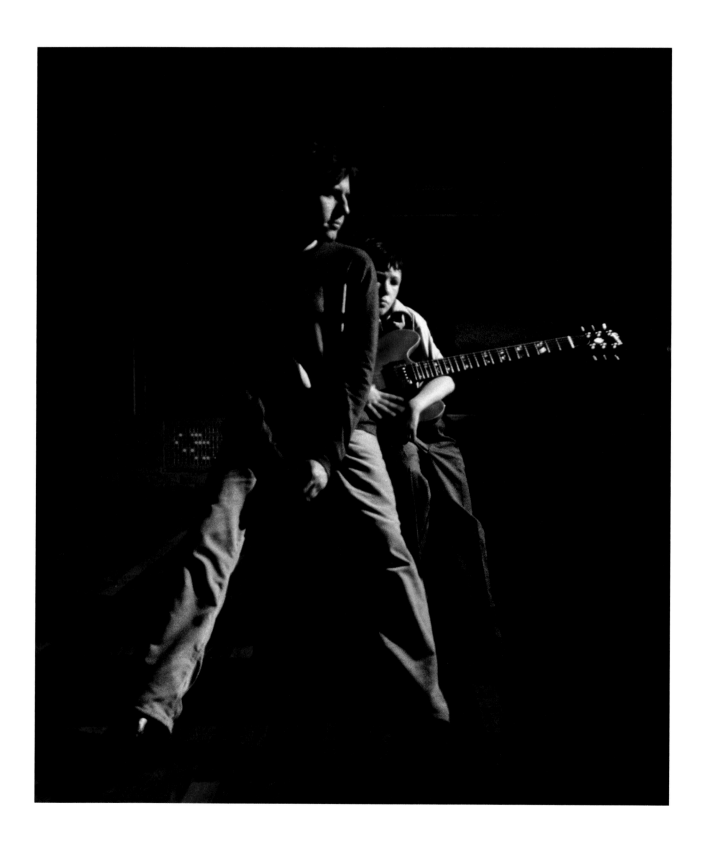

1.   What is Hard-core?

2.   What's your earliest TV memory?

3.   Did your parents ration TV?

4   Have you ever learnt anything from TV?

5.   Have you ever watched a dirty video?
    i.   Did you enjoy it?
    ii.   Would you watch with your partner?
    iii.   Would you be in one?

6.   Have you ever been photographed in the nude?

7.   Are you frightened of getting old?

8.   What will this century be remembered for?

9.   Who's the most famous person in the world, of this century?

10.   Would you like to be famous?

11.   What do you think being famous is like?

12.   What would you do with the power?

13.   What are you frightened of?

14.   Have you ever had a panic attack?

15.   Do you believe in Jesus/any religion?

16.   Do you believe in life after death?

17.   What's the best party you have ever been to?

18.   What's the most drunk you've ever been?

19.   What have you most regretted doing at a party?

20.   Have you ever had an older/younger lover?

21.   Have you ever sniffed glue?

22.   Have you ever loved and lost?

23.   Did your parents stay together?

24.   Have you got/do you want children?

25.   What is soul?

26.   Do people have a soul?

27.   When did you feel you had become an adult?

28.   Will men and women ever be equal?

29.   Have you got a favourite chat up line?

30.   Would you like to go out with someone who is famous?

31.   Who was the first famous person you fancied?

32.   What's your best/worst physical feature?

33.   Are good looking people happier than ugly ones?

34.   What do you think of anorexia?

35.   Have you ever gone out with someone because they reminded you of somebody famous that you fancied?

36.   Have you ever been unemployed? If so, how did you fill your days?

37.   What's the proudest moment of your life?

38.   Do you believe in astrology?

39.   When was your lowest ebb?

40.   Have you ever considered suicide?

41.   What's the most rebellious thing you've ever done?

42.   Are you political?

43.   What one thing would you most like to change in your life/world?

44.   Is world peace a possibility?

45.   Is there life on other planets?

46.   Where will you be on New Year's Eve 1999?

Paul Burgess and Litsa Aris were asked to make part of a behind-the-scenes documentary on 24 April 1998 on set at Olympic Studios. Jarvis wrote out 46 questions related to the themes of the *This Is Hardcore* album, and these questions were put to the child actors, make-up artist, stylists, canteen staff and the director. The 16mm film remains unseen at the time of writing.

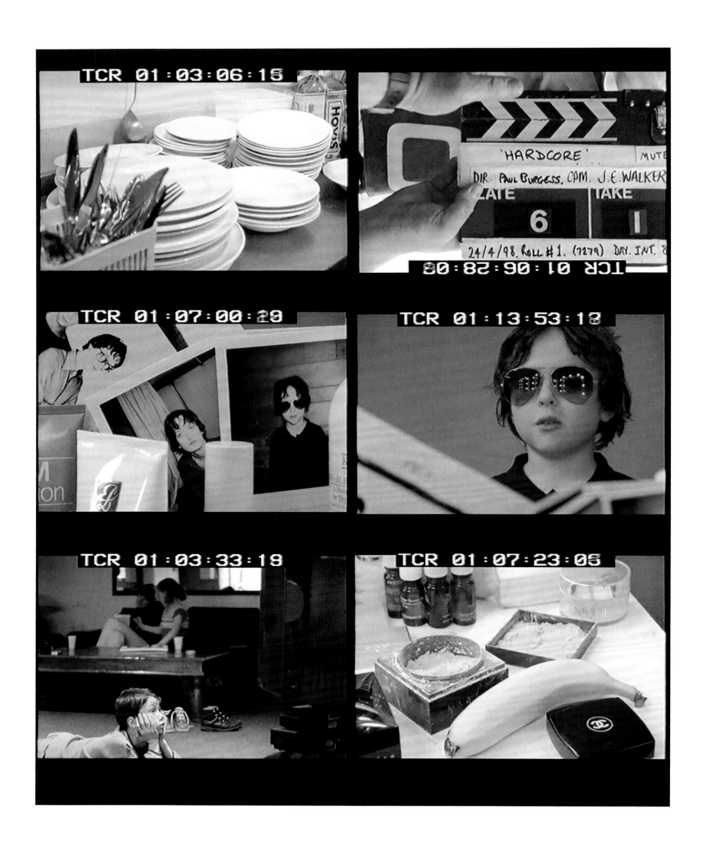

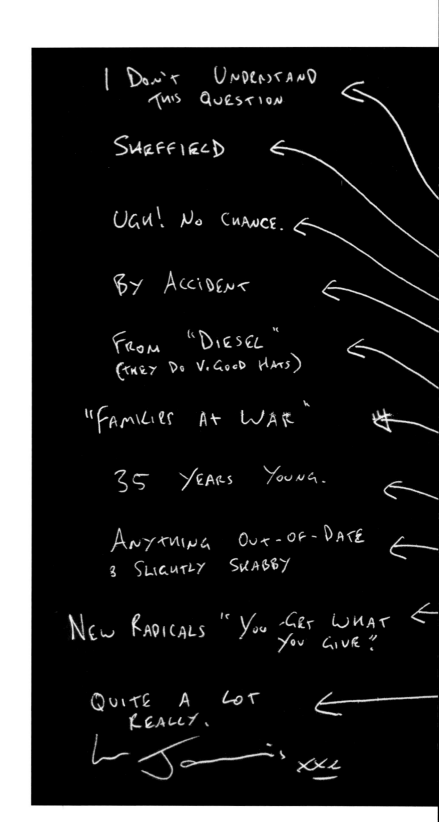

A list of questions given to Jarvis in 1998
by Lily Rose Dawes (then aged 12).

a few questions I would like
to know abat {pop}
because I love
to sing!

thank you !

1. do you go to those chats at tea time !
2. where do you come from
3. do you have ~~coming~~ any piercings!
4. how did you become a pop star!
5. where did you get your hat from !
6. I like eastenders, what programme do you like
7. how old are you
8. what kind! of fashone do you like
9. what is your best song you bort at lately
10. do you eat much

> if youve got the time

147

CANDIDA DOYLE

In conversation with Paul Burgess (PB)

It's the 21st of December 2022 – the shortest day of the year – when I meet Candida Doyle at her home in Stoke Newington, London. I begin by asking what she's been up to in the years since Pulp's last live show in 2012.

CD   I bought a cottage in the Shetland Islands, where my family comes from. It's beautiful, it's just next to a hill, it's in the village where most of my Shetland family live and that's just bliss. I trained to be a counsellor – a counsellor as in a therapist, not as in the government. I've been doing that at a charity place in Hackney and just living the life of Riley really, I can pretty much please myself. I take very well to that way of life. I'm very happy.

PB   How often do you go up to the Shetland Islands?

CD   I try to go three or four times a year but COVID made that difficult. I was meant to go in October 2022, and then I thought I would have to stay and rehearse because I've been rehearsing on my own before getting together with everyone.

PB   Didn't Pulp once play on Shetland?

CD   Yeah, we did, but there's no way that will happen again. I think I wouldn't be allowed and I kind of want to keep it separate – my Shetland life to Pulp, you know?

PB   I remember you always being very quiet, and not around a great deal on the video sets. I spent more time with Mark, Steve, Jarvis and Nick. I don't remember you being in the dressing room very much. I think you must have gone somewhere else.

CD   Possibly, yeah (laughing). I was not very happy in the whole 'Hardcore' time, so I probably did everything slightly grudgingly, I would imagine, and anything extra I would flee from if I could.

PB   Let's wind back to 1997. After twelve months of touring *Different Class*, how ready did you feel to begin writing and recording *This Is Hardcore*?

CD   Not at all ready. By the end of touring *Different Class*, it was all fine until I had this huge panic attack in Germany and then it just gave me 'the fear'. Then, of course, we go writing an LP all about the fear and freaking out, which didn't really help. I needed to do nothing to do with Pulp for a year – ideally, this is what I would have liked – because that fear of the panic attacks lasted for another year or so. Then when we did go out on tour in 1998, I was apprehensive. I thought, shit, what's it going to be like? And then Richard Hawley came on board, Russell Senior had left – Russell leaving was quite disconcerting and part of me thought, if Russell's going, then I think I'm going to go. I stayed but I did think 'I've had it'.

PB   Was it anxiety about performing live particularly, or was it general anxiety?

CD   Just generally, I felt very ungrounded. I remember being at my parent's house [but] I still felt weird and I thought, 'God, if you feel weird at your parent's house…' I just felt total stress and burnout. I don't like that word, 'burnout', it sounds too American – but I had it. The final thing was, as you can imagine, the excitement around *Different Class* and going to America for the first time. It was just such an incredibly high-octane excitement. We had three weeks in America, we came back for three days and then went to do three weeks in Germany and I think that was the mistake. If that hadn't happened, maybe I would have carried on really enjoying it but after that I just went off it.

PB   How much did you miss the presence of Russell following his departure in January 1997 and how did it change the dynamic of the band?

CD   Russell was quite a big presence. He just didn't feel it was realistic that we should be singing about 'common people' when we weren't common people anymore. There had been some kind of conflict with him and Jarvis, and Russell could be difficult. But when he left I was a bit sad because I wasn't feeling steady in myself anyway. So, for him to go, it made me [feel] even less grounded because he was in the group before I joined. I [then] became the longest standing member apart from Jarvis, but maybe the atmosphere was a bit easier without Russell.

PB   So, when you started work on *This Is Hardcore*, and when it came out, what was your reaction to it as an album? It seemed to have fewer prominent keyboard or synth parts and a slightly more guitar-based sound.

CD   Right. I didn't even notice, and I love guitars, so yeah, I didn't notice because when we play live, a lot of those sounds have gone onto my keyboards – so I still do a lot in it. To be honest, I don't listen to our records that much. I really don't. It's kind of weird because I know it's a good album and I've had to listen to the songs lately just to remember what I did on them for this tour. And yeah, it all feels a bit, not vain, but a little bit self-indulgent – maybe that's what it is. My neighbour upstairs is a Pulp fan, so I never want him to know I am playing my own songs. I can hear his music through the floorboards. Sometimes I've played us live just to see what I did but I keep it down; I don't need him to know.

PB   Several bands around in the late 90s seemed to find success with darker-sounding albums. Particularly Radiohead, Blur, Portishead and even Supergrass. Did this make you feel more confident about the direction Pulp was taking with *This Is Hardcore*? Because obviously it's quite a shift, isn't it, from *Different Class*.

CD   In 1998 I did have the LPs of those contemporary artists. Portishead, The Verve, Radiohead and Blur. I did like them all but I wasn't affected at all by what everyone else was doing. I wasn't going home listening to Pulp either. Usually, I listen to a lot of 1970s stuff. A lot of Black music. Do you know that *This is Soul* LP? I love that LP and Stevie Wonder. I listened to a lot of American Black music and 70s disco, good 70s disco – not crap. Also, classical music. Well, most music, but I don't like hip hop and I don't like heavy metal.

PB   Do you ever listen to any kind of Moog-based music or anything that's keyboard- or synthesizer-based? Or even just piano records or keyboard records? You are not a secret Rick Wakeman fan then?

CD   No, God, no way! I like some classical piano, though.

PB   *This Is Hardcore* seemed to take a long time to create, with most of the songs only nearing completion in the late summer of 1997, eight months before the album's release. With popular music tastes starting to shift, did you ever think *This Is Hardcore*'s time might pass before it was released? Can you tell me about the writing process at 'The Fortress', which was a pretty horrible rehearsal space I gather?

CD   It was really horrible. It just did not help the whole atmosphere of the LP. Just thinking about that period makes me feel ill. It was a dark room; I think Primal Scream used it. It [was] really dark and it just felt very druggy – I just didn't want anything to do with that. I wanted to try and feel clear and pure and get back to myself and it just didn't help at all. No windows, just 12pm–6pm writing these heavy songs. Yeah! It was dark, dark times.

PB   It's interesting. I bumped into Jarvis at the exhibition for his book and he spent quite some time showing me around and explaining what everything was, which was very good of him. Toward the end we were talking a little bit about this book, and I said, what do you remember from the *Hardcore* period? He replied, 'I can't remember very much at all from that period of my life.' So, I don't know whether he was having a hard time as well back then.

CD   Oh, that makes me feel better, at least I can remember some of it. I just don't remember it pleasantly.

PB   Let's move on to something a bit lighter. Aside from the writing of the album I wonder if you had any memories about the making of the four music videos? There was 'Help the Aged', which was filmed in Stoke Newington Town Hall. That is the video with the Stannah stairlift and a scene based on the film *A Matter of Life and Death*. Did you know that Kelly Brook was in that video? She's one of the female actors in the back of the video, with dark hair. It was one of her first jobs when she was in her 20s.

CD   In 'Help the Aged'? I can only remember Jarvis coming up the stairs on that video on the stairlift.

CD   I was very pleased that I could just walk there and walk back, and usually I was just getting taxis to West London for anything Pulp. So, I liked that it was local in Stoke Newington. I couldn't believe it was just up the road, really, because nothing was happening here at the time.

PB   One of the men in the 'Help the Aged' video is Pat Skinny. You know, your stylist? He was wearing a fake beard.

CD   Oh, yes. I remember. I got on well with Pat and Jo.

PB   Moving on to 'This Is Hardcore', one of the things Louise and I loved when we first emailed you, was your comment about being styled with the red dress and the make-up. You said you hated it. Could you tell me how that video felt to make and a bit more about being made up in a 1950s-style red cocktail dress.

CD   I just hated the look I was given. The hair, the dress, everything! I love the song and video but I was always my own stylist and would wear my own clothes in Pulp and, so, to be dressed by a stylist felt very fake. It felt against everything I believed Pulp to be. I think at that point. It feels bad to say, but I almost begrudged anything 'Pulp' that I had to do. I'd been in this long-term relationship with Pete, who used to play bass in the group before I joined. He would never have asked me to leave and I would never have left for him but I think that, deep down, he found Pulp's success very difficult. So, neither of us were in a good way. I wasn't going to leave, but I was not feeling myself. I don't know if I was at Pinewood much, I wasn't there every day. I know that I missed the stuff with the girls and the feathers and all that. And I do regret that because that must have been so good. Steve was even saying 'you've got to watch this, it's just amazing'. But any chance or excuse of not having to be there, I just wouldn't be there. So, unfortunately, I missed that. And I think at that time, like being given this red dress to wear and being 'styled', I just kind of handed myself over and let it be done because obviously that was how it was going to be. Maybe I was just a bit lost with where Pulp had gone and where I'd gone a little bit. But it's when I look back and I think, fuck. I always prided myself on not having a stylist, I think, in a few of those videos, like the 'This Is Hardcore' video, I'm styled and it's like ughhhh – hate it!

PB   And how do you feel when you look at the 'This Is Hardcore' video now?

CD   Yeah, well, I'm surprised how much I'm in it. I really thought I was not in it much at all but my part is quite long. The other guys do a bit of acting. I just feel like I can't act. Nick, he's a natural, even Mark and Steve – all of them. If I'd been told to do something other than play piano, I don't know how that would have been. I just can't do it.

PB   The next video was 'A Little Soul', which is very different. It was filmed in Olympic Studios – the recording studio. I like to think of it as the 'mahogany' video because there's a lot of wood everywhere and Jarvis is wearing a brown shirt. The video had child actors – you had a great mini-Candida actor playing the part of you as a child. It's quite a simple video so you would have been there for one day, I'm guessing, filming the scene where you're sat at the piano with the child version of yourself playing the keys. At the beginning, you are wheeled in on a sofa by mini-Candida.

CD   I'm wheeled in, yeah. I don't really remember anything about 'A Little Soul' except feeling that, because the girl was dressed in the kind of clothes that I do usually wear and on that day I wasn't, I did feel that I'd let them down a bit – but I didn't know that was going to happen. I don't particularly like the song that much. I didn't really feel that my heart was in it.

PB   It is obviously very much a song Jarvis wrote about his relationship with his father.

CD   I know, it's very revealing. I think it's very brave of him to bare his soul so directly in the song because, obviously, a lot of the songs are about people but that one is so clearly about his dad. It's like, wow.

PB   The final video, which presumably was a bit more upbeat for you, is 'Party Hard'. This is the one directed by Mike Mills, another American director. There were lots of red balloons and you stand on a white cube playing your keyboard at the back, while about 20 dancers do cartwheels.

CD   It's not bringing up any good memories. I hate 'Party Hard'.

PB   You don't like that song? Or the video?

CD   I hate it. Nothing about it appeals to me. I don't like the melody and I don't like what I play in it. But the girls were lovely, they were really great fun.

PB   The girls were from Pineapple Studios, the dance studio. They were exhausted – I mean, they were doing cartwheels for hours – because there were so many takes. It was just amazing to witness their stamina.

CD   Oh my God. Yeah, they were amazing.

PB   So can I ask you one final question to do with videos? What you've said with these four videos is that you didn't really enjoy the process of making them. Can you remember the last time you did enjoy making a Pulp video where you came away and just went, that was fun, I really enjoyed that and you liked the result as well? Because before *This Is Hardcore* it would have been things like 'Mis-shapes', 'Common People' and 'Disco 2000'.

CD   'Razzmatazz' was quite fun, because we were in a hotel in Paris and it was all quite new to us, and 'Babies' – both of those videos were good because it was all still quite light then. And 'Common People', I just play my bit. I think it's funny that I am uncomfortable in front of the camera and yet I want to be filmed. I want to

be as much part of it as everyone else. But the actual thing of being filmed I don't like. For photo sessions, I just have to drink alcohol before and then when I pose for a picture I dig my nail hard into my hand so I don't blink, otherwise I could just get distracted. It's weird, actually, all the extra things I'd have to do with Pulp – I didn't really like photo sessions or videos but I liked doing in-store signings because we would get free CDs. We'd get five free CDs and we were still quite skint then, so any of that was really exciting. But I'm discovering more and more that there's a lot of it I didn't like.

PB   I just remembered another time when I did meet you briefly to take some photos, when Pulp did a signing for 'Help the Aged' at HMV in 1997. Jarvis, Steve and Martin Green were DJing and loads of Pulp fans queued up to have things signed.

CD   It was very heady days.

PB   Do you have a favourite song from the *Hardcore* album? You've talked about some that you don't like?

CD   Well there is one I do love, 'TV Movie', I really like that one. I also love 'This Is Hardcore'. I just get goosebumps, even playing it live. Some of the chord changes are just beautiful.

PB   The song 'This Is Hardcore' famously has a wonderful sample from 'Bolero on the Moon Rocks' by Peter Thomas Sound Orchester. Can you remember whose idea it was to use that? Because, at the time, Steve was experimenting with a lot of samples and loops.

CD   I'd say Jarvis or Steve would have found it. I remember they were playing the loop in the rehearsal room, I had just been to the toilet and I was coming down the stairs and heard the track and I thought, oh, that's going to be really light and breezy and then it really wasn't. I remember thinking, oh, yeah, it's refreshing and then it was really heavy.

PB   Several years after *This Is Hardcore* was first released, Island Records re-released it as a deluxe CD with lots of B-sides and demos of songs that were recorded at the time but didn't make it onto the album. Some of these songs were heading down more of an electronica path. Do you think, in retrospect, the right songs were included on the original release? Some great songs weren't included, there's a song called 'It's A Dirty World'. 'The Professional' that was on the B-side of 'A Little Soul' and then, of course, 'Cocaine Socialism', which later became 'Glory Days'.

CD   'We are the Boyz', is that on the re-released LP? 'We are the Boyz' – I love that song. I don't feel that [the B-sides] should have been on the album, though, because I think it does work as an LP and there's some songs that would have shaken that balance. Although 'Cocaine Socialism' is so exciting... I think Jarvis just felt bad about releasing it.

PB   Did you write the music together as a group for *This Is Hardcore* and was it an easy or difficult writing process?

CD   Yes, we did write the music together as a group, and yes, it was difficult. Jarvis starts by kind of mumbling a melody and then the lyrics usually come at the end. I'd say the tune comes first. We usually do lots of little bits of songs and then we put them together and create a song out of bits of songs.

PB   Looking back at the time you spent in the studio creating *This Is Hardcore*, you were working with Chris Thomas – who you worked with on *Different Class*. Can you say what he's like? Was his approach different across the two albums?

CD   I don't remember much but he was completely different to Scott Walker who produced *We Love Life*. Chris would like us all to be there in the studio and he'd regale us with great stories of his career because, obviously, he's lived. Whereas with Scott Walker, it felt like he didn't really want any of us there and he wouldn't tell you any stories. He would only want the one person there that's doing their bit. But, yeah, he was very 'he's got his beret on' and that was it.

PB   Which did you prefer? Just purely as a producer?

CD   I liked them both, but in different ways. Chris Thomas is a party man whereas, with Scott Walker, you could maybe sit and read a book with him or something. I only discovered recently that when he toured with the Walker Brothers, Jimmy Hendrix played on the same tour – I would've loved to have asked him about that, but I didn't know at the time. I was never a Scott Walker fan. The rest of the group were all like, oh, my God, it's Scott Walker, and I was not really fussed. Scott was a nice man, but Chris Thomas was great. He did the Sex Pistols and Roxy Music, and he was an engineer on The Beatles's *White Album*. I felt Chris Thomas captured the energy of us as we were when we played live on stage and I thought we were always better live – which never got onto record until Chris Thomas.

PB   Pulp always seemed to be a very democratic group. There are five (formerly six) equal members and, as far as I know, the money and song writing credits are spilt evenly amongst you. How did this affect the way you worked together in a positive or negative way?

CD   Well it kept a balance of fairness within the group relationship and I think different people add different qualities to a band; one member may not be so involved in the writing of a song, but their genial temperament helps create a good ambience within the group dynamics, which is important. I am not referring to anyone in particular there!

PB   What memories, if any, do you have of the *Hardcore* album launch party when Pulp played in the ballroom at the top of the Hilton Hotel. It was a pink and black dress code, very swanky. It was the first time Pulp played the new *This Is Hardcore* songs live. We have got some photographs of it in the book.

CD   Oh, my God. It was full of doom and gloom, I hated it. Fucking hated it! I hated the whole atmosphere around *This Is Hardcore*. It just felt so opposite to who I am, the thought of it makes my skin crawl. It was quite druggy. Yeah, that night it felt quite druggy. There was a kind of fake glam, with the actor guy from the album sleeve walking around and just how all that plastic-ness kind of made my skin crawl. I suppose we were a bit unsure because it was very different to *Different Class*. Not good memories. Posh – really posh. But despite disliking the Hilton event and finding it fake at the time, I now look at our history with that hotel with pride. As I go past the hotel now, I think, wow, we had that whole top room.

PB   You have a strong sense of your own style. Can you say if and how you think you influenced the overall look of the Pulp aesthetic over the years? It is a difficult thing to talk about but people talk about the Pulp style, the Pulp look, and I guess in the early to mid 90s, around the time of *His 'n' Hers*, it very much would have been your 70s references and your jumble sale, charity shop clothing and everything like that. I'm starting to detect that maybe one of the reasons you hated the *This Is Hardcore* period is because all of that was just pulled away and you were suddenly styled by others. It was odd for many at this time, to see Jarvis in magazines wearing Gucci belts and Diesel jackets.

CD   Yeah. I think that's where Russell struggled. The weird thing is, when you get famous you start getting free clothes – which really doesn't make sense to me whatsoever, because it should be the other way around. When you've got loads of money, you don't need free clothes, but people want you to wear their stuff. I suppose with *Different Class* we weren't famous, we could just do it and we were kind of left alone. By the time of *This Is Hardcore*, we were famous and Diesel wanted us to go and film in their shops or wear their clothes, or Island Records wanted us to do a promo film – just weird stuff. I suppose we did it because we had never done that kind of thing before but it wasn't healthy, I would say. With my own look, I did have my stripy tops and suede miniskirts and that kind of thing and, the funny thing is, as I lost my love of being in Pulp, I noticed that Pulp fans were looking more like Pulp than we were. They really got it, yet we were kind of not looking so 'Pulp' for a time.

PB   How did you feel when it moved on to the *We Love Life* tour and when you were playing in places like the Eden Project? Playing in forests and Jarvis sang in just bare feet and often sporting an Arran knit jumper.

CD   Yeah, it all went nice again. Back to nature. I was happier with *We Love Life*. That's the funny thing, the happier we were, the less potent our music was.

PB   It's only my personal memories from being on those four video sets but I remember a lot of fun, I didn't see any drugs and I didn't hear anyone talking about being miserable.

CD   It wasn't solemn?

PB   No, the only time I remember it being solemn – because I spent a lot of time in the dressing room on the 'This is Hardcore' set at Pinewood, just waiting around – was one afternoon when Jarvis and Jeannette were in the dressing room and the radio was on playing 'This Is Hardcore' for the very first time. Jarvis just sat there through the entire track, smoking a cigarette. He had an empty can of Coke in his hand and he was tapping the ash into it – deep in thought. He sat silently all through the whole song, he particularly wanted to hear what the bass sounded like and how it came across sonically on a little tiny radio, and he was completely focused on how it sounded.

CD   He has got amazing ears, Jarvis.

PB   I think Steve was in the room as well. There was discussion about bass frequencies and could they push up the levels on the mastering. I think the BBC must have been playing an acetate or something. On the last day at Pinewood, they shot the video for 'Like a Friend' on the 'This Is Hardcore' set. I have a video I filmed of Jarvis messing around, playing drums, dancing, rolling on the floor and just having a laugh – letting off steam. It was included on the 'Home Movies' extras on the *Pulp Hits* DVD. There were definitely fun times going on during the 'This Is Hardcore' shoot, maybe it just wasn't as evident as it was before.

CD   I don't think it was depressing for everyone. I don't know if Nick found it hard. I don't know if Steve did or Mark, but I know I did and I know Jarvis did. I think I just wanted a year off, a break. But I can see that if you disappear, you can be forgotten and you've got to keep going. I can see that now, but it was a chore.

PB   My memories of Nick were just upbeat, reading the newspaper and keeping chipper. I remember Mark mostly reading books on experimental filmmaking from the 1960s. He gave me a pre-release cassette of the *Hardcore* album at Pinewood, it was so great to hear it before anyone else.

PB   I was interested to see Camille Bidault-Waddington's name on the album, as the stylist on the *This Is Hardcore* album cover.

CD   Yes, she styled the photographs that are taken at the Hilton by Horst [Diekgerdes]. So, again, photographs of me and they are not my clothes. I think this is roughly around the time Jarvis and Camille met each other. I like Camille, she's really nice and she approached me very gently. She is quite ahead of her time, fashion-wise. Stylist is almost the wrong word for her, she is more of an artist in some way.

PB   What are your memories from that photo shoot at the Hilton?

CD   Just not great. I hate sounding so down on it all again but I think I found it hard. I just had a natural distrust of people in the music business, or even the styling business. I think my roots are very earthy, coming from Shetland, living in Sheffield and then suddenly finding it all really posh with lots of people telling you what to do. I mean, everyone was nice but I just found it all very fake and I found the music industry very fake. I found it very hard to meet genuine people when Pulp got big and I really like genuine people. There were a few genuine people around during the whole *This Is Hardcore* time, like the Rough Trade gang. Obviously, it was so big, and we were up there, but I wasn't at home in that situation.

PB   There is much more of a gender balance within the music industry these days – was it difficult being a woman in such a male dominated environment back in the 1990s?

CD   It didn't feel difficult being the only female. It's just how it was. I can only recall a couple of situations where I felt awkward about being female. I had grown up with two brothers, so I was quite at home in male company. Part of the reason I stayed in Pulp, if I occasionally considered leaving, was because women were so rarely represented in bands then – so I felt that I had to show women they have a place there!

PB   Do you have a favourite gig that Pulp played on the *This Is Hardcore* tour? And what do you remember of the big Finsbury Park Pulp concert? Finsbury Park was a sort of 'Pulpstock', wasn't it? It was your own festival in a field in London.

CD   Yeah. That was exciting because, obviously, it's walking distance from my house... Finsbury Park was generally okay and enjoyable and I love playing outside. I can't remember the support bands but I think it was Catatonia and my mate's band, Bikini Beach – they played. There were a few bands that played. Having Richard Hawley on tour with us was a lot of fun. Going to Australia and New Zealand was very exciting. Australia was amazing, it felt weird that they speak English because it felt so foreign to me. I thought they should speak some exotic language. It was the first time we went to Japan too. I was quite scared of going that far because I don't like flying and I didn't know how I was going to get through the 24-hour flight. I found this book on patchwork and I thought, perfect, I can do that. When it's turbulent and you're reading a book, you stop reading and you think, oh, my God, I'm going to die. Whereas a patchwork, you can sew through it. You can sew through the fear. I would go and buy material for patchworks when we went to foreign places. I had got a side project on the go.

PB   By the time the *This Is Hardcore* tour finished in December 1998, the future of the band seemed more uncertain than at any other time since the late 80s. What made you go on and record the final album and obviously do a much more enjoyable tour playing in all the forests? Was it just having some time off?

CD   I think when we toured in 1998, we put something like a month's gap in between tours. We certainly did stuff so that it would not seem so horrendous. We finished the *This Is Hardcore* tour at the end of '98.

PB   Presumably there was a nice break before starting to write the final album and getting Scott Walker involved?

CD   Yeah. I think we must have just thought we had more songs or something, or we didn't want to end it like that. I remember having a conversation in a taxi with Jarvis and deciding the next LP would be the last one. I can't say we all felt happy but I certainly felt happier by that point. It just felt more real. We had gone so synthetic, or plastic, which I can see we kind of needed to explore for This Is Hardcore and that was the aim. But I hated it.

PB   It's interesting when you ask Pulp fans, which albums they love the most, they nearly always say, *This Is Hardcore* and *Different Class*, and obviously the older fans, *His 'n' Hers*. But it's surprising how high up the top of the list *This Is Hardcore* is. I think it feels like a substantial piece of art, really. We'll talk a bit about the cover in a minute. But it's got the Peter Saville artwork, it caught everyone's attention.

CD   God, the artwork.

PB   There are two broad perspectives on how to view *This Is Hardcore* twenty-five years on. Either as a dark and claustrophobic comedown album, after the excess of the mid 90s, or as a more optimistic tale of redemption and survival following hardship – a light at the end of the tunnel. Looking back, which of the two different perspectives do you think resonates the strongest with you?

CD   Definitely the first one, I don't see it as light or redemption.

PB   Because it's often talked about as being a sort of comedown album after the dreaded words 'Brit Pop', which I know no one likes at all and I don't like either. *This Is Hardcore* is often referred to as the antithesis to all that.

CD   It feels a bit like Dr Jekyll and Mr Hyde. *Different Class* is Dr Jekyll, *This Is Hardcore* is Mr Hyde.

PB   Jarvis has announced recently in the press that he's writing the second part of his autobiography. I think Nick's writing a book as well. But it'd be very interesting to see how Jarvis approaches the *This Is Hardcore* period in his book, what he writes about and how he writes about it.

CD   Will he be able to put in much? I mean, it is hard. I've seen him in interviews speak about fame, saying he doesn't want to be negative about the great opportunity but he likens it to being allergic to nuts – I feel the same way. It doesn't feel good to speak so negatively about something that was amazing. I can see they're good songs. I might not like them all, but I can see that they're good.

PB   There are three songs on that album, particularly, that are certainly up there in my top four or five Pulp songs. 'This Is Hardcore', 'Seductive Barry' and 'The Fear'.

CD   That is one of the things I found really hard, because when we played live, we were behind a screen and I'd go out, be the first one on stage, behind the screen,

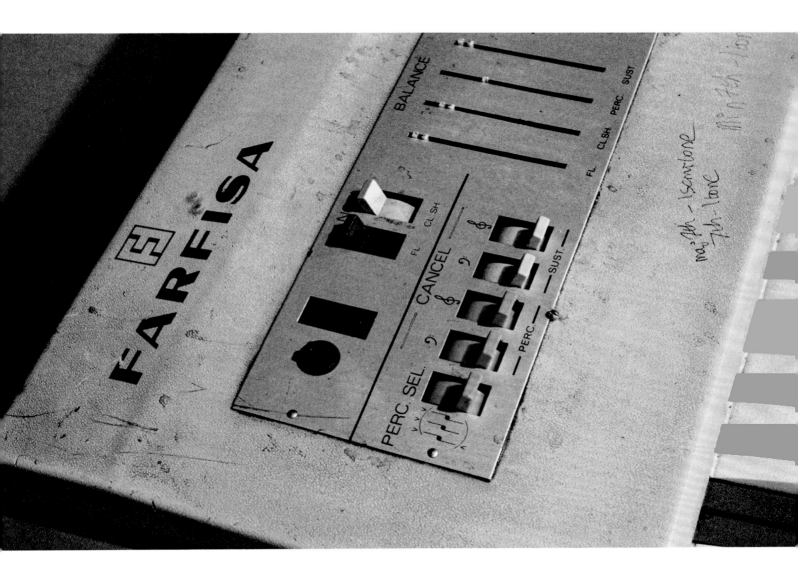

and I'd have to play the 'neeeer, neeeer' beginning of 'The Fear' and it was the last thing I wanted to do. I don't want to play that song. I hate it. It gives me the fear and I've got to go out and do it on my own. Jarvis was actually very sweet because he told me to think about the two references to food in it. One is something about having a laugh, a 'falafel' and what's the other one? I think he was trying to help me get through doing something that he saw I very clearly did not want to do, and he was so sweet. What's the other one? Taco, panic attack-o! Panic attack – it became a taco. I just thought, what if I go on stage and I just run off again or something?

PB   What do you feel most proud about *This Is Hardcore*?

CD   'This Is Hardcore' does stand up as one of our best songs.

PB   What's your take, Candida, on what the lyrics are about?

CD   Oh, God. The song is delving into the darkest side of life and dabbling with porn and drugs – the seedy side of life. That makes me think of *The Portrait of Dorian Gray*, the side that was hidden on the portrait, that is what comes to my mind. Not mother nature (laughs).

PB   What were the other songs from *This Is Hardcore* that you remember feeling really excited about once you'd finished writing them? Did you feel differently about any songs when you began playing them to a live audience?

CD   If I didn't like a song when we wrote it then, usually, I still didn't like it when we recorded, mixed it or played it live. If I really liked one of our songs, then I liked it even more when we played it live; so possibly the songs I didn't like, I hated more as we played them live. 'The Fear' – I never liked it much but I just listened to the live at Finsbury Park version and I really like it now, waddya know! I'm glad. 'Dishes' – always loved it, always will. 'Party Hard' – never liked it and still don't! 'Help the Aged' – loved it straight away and still do. 'This Is Hardcore' – one of our very best. 'TV Movie' – love it. 'A Little Soul' – I quite like it. 'I'm A Man' – I love it, then and now. 'Seductive Barry' – I don't really enjoy this one... It was written partly in tribute to Barry White. 'Sylvia' – not a fan. 'Glory Days' – I love. I was disappointed when 'Cocaine Socialism' turned into this, but I still love it! 'The Day After The Revolution' – a good ending.

PB   I'd like to talk a little bit about the cover of the *This Is Hardcore* album. Did you think at the time the cover design was challenging? Did you like it at the time? And do you like it now?

CD   I've never liked it and I don't think I ever will. I think I must have split my mind from it, it had gone into a whole area I just didn't even get – so I just didn't really have anything to do with it.

PB   Do you remember how you felt when you saw it for the first time?

CD   Yeah, I was shocked. I met the girl who was on the cover, Ksenia, wasn't it? She shaved her arms so as not to have any body hair. Everything about it made me cringe. It was so plastic, which I know it was meant to be. Looking back, I think, fuck, I could have got on a really feminist thing there and said – what the fuck are you doing? But I just let it be because it had gone into a realm that I didn't understand and didn't want to understand. So that's just how it is. I didn't get involved with the covers. I would say I like the 'Mis-shapes' single cover; it was like a sewing kind of pattern and we were all drawn. Yeah, I really like that.

PB   I think at that time Jarvis was living in a place in Maida Vale, he had a sort of Playboy flat for a while. Maybe that inspired the cover?

CD   It was in Edgeware Road. Yeah, it was really big and funky. I remember Jarvis's flat having a TV with a lot of channels because – at that point – we still only had five, and it had all the channels. I think the flat cost a hell of a lot of money. But then we did have a hell of a lot of money. Jarvis lived in Peckham or Camberwell earlier on, so I could see why he would want to upgrade.

PB   I've got a couple of press cuttings from *The Independent* newspaper at the time when the *Hardcore* album came out, criticising the cover as it was fly-posted around London and on the Underground.

CD   Yeah, it was on buses.

PB   A lot of people wrote graffiti on it, saying, 'this degrades women' and *The Independent* did an article about it. Then some of the readers wrote in and said, 'no, we love the album cover, you're obviously missing Jarvis's point that it is about what happens to people when they get used up.' Presumably it was chosen as an image to cause some controversy?

CD   Yeah, Jarvis just liked to do that and I can see he wasn't doing it in a sexist way. He was showing the sleazy side of the hardcore life.

PB   As someone who used to be an avid viewer of Top of the Pops, do you remember how you felt performing 'This Is Hardcore' on the show in March 1998.

CD   I don't remember performing 'This is Hardcore' on TOTP!

PB   What sort of music do you listen to now, if any?

CD   Let me see... If I had to do Desert Island Discs... There is a band I like at the moment, actually, called the Oracle Sisters. I'm trying to get them to play with us on our tour but I don't know if I can. They're kind of light and breezy. I like melodic stuff and harmonies. But then, I like Tchaikovsky and Mozart, and some folk music, as well as bluegrass, a lot of Black music, Scottish country music and 70s disco. I like ABBA and some Elton John. I quite like chilled music. But I also like high-octane music like 'Born Slippy' [Underworld] or some of

Moby's LPs – a real variety. I think Pulp fans might be surprised by what I listen to because it doesn't feel like it's what a Pulp fan would listen to and I am a Pulp fan.

PB   Do you still have your beautiful Farfisa organ and will you be using it on the tour?

CD   Yes, it was here in the flat last week. It was beautiful, it's pretty battered now. I've got a recent picture of it here because, to set it up, we had to use four cobblestones, 2G clamps and some weird things to get it at the right height. But yeah, it will be coming on tour with me.

PB   Are you excited about the upcoming tour? Both you and Jarvis are going to turn 60 at some point during the year.

CD   Yes, me before him!

PB   Will there be any new Pulp music?

CD   No, I don't think that's a good idea. I mean, Jarvis has his other band. If he wants to write songs, he can do that. It's funny because, before, when we were still existing as a band, in between playing our songs, someone would mess about and then it would turn into a new song. But now, when we rehearse, we don't do anything like that. We don't veer toward the possibility of writing new songs at all. I just don't think it's a good idea.

PB   I know you're not going to tell me any of the songs you're doing, but have any surprised you?

CD   There's been some surprises but we have all got an opportunity to put forward some songs that we really like to do and then we'll try it out. Some will work, some won't.

PB   Thanks Candida, that's everything. Do you think there's anything I've not asked you that you would like to have written in the book?

CD   No, I'd like to be a bit more positive. I certainly enjoyed going to foreign places on the *This Is Hardcore* tour.

PB   Well that is a happy ending to finish on.

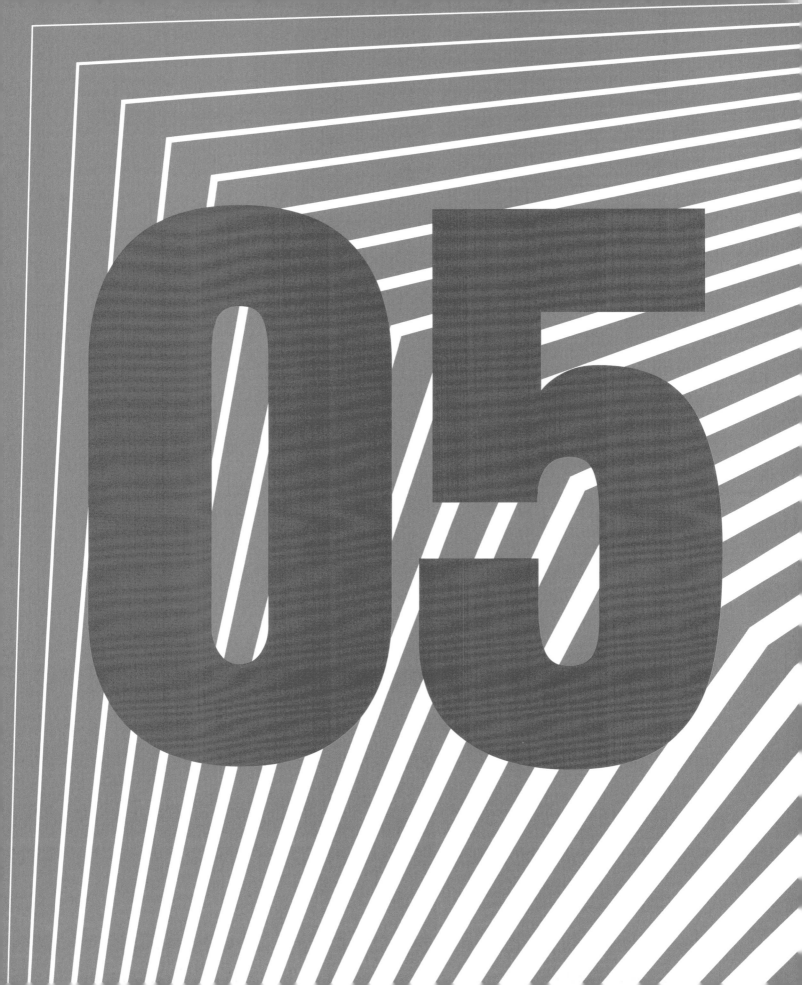

Director: Mike Mills
Produced by: Nick Landon
Shoot Date: 7 August 1998
Location: Asylum Studios, 1 Wadsworth Close,
Perivale, Middlesex, UB6 7DG

Released on the 7 September 1998, 'Party Hard' was the fourth single taken from *This Is Hardcore*. It reached number 29 in the charts.

The music video was directed by Mike Mills. The inspiration for the video came from an obscure 1970s German TV show *Männer wir kommen!* – which translates as 'Men, we are coming!'. The costume and set designs were created by the artist Allen Jones. The TV show was produced by WDR (Westdeutscher Rundfunk), Cologne, and directed by Bob Rooyens. There are also graphical similarities between the 'Party Hard' music video and the film *Mr. Freedom* (1968) directed by William Klein.

The set was alive with pops of colour from red balloons, contrasted with the white cubes used as futuristic plinths for the members of Pulp and their instruments. The dancers were from Pineapple and Success Dance Studios, the dog T-shirts they wore were a happy shade of blue-sky blue and the sweatbands on their wrists coupled with white striped trainers called to mind cheerleaders from the 1980s brought into the pop-art sensibility of the 1990s. The backlighting created huge bursting stars of light on the black backdrop. Electric boogaloo, endless cartwheels, white on red love hearts, glitter raining down – all combined to impart the message: have fun now and suffer later.

Jarvis wearing black sandals and hugging a big red balloon, POP! Dogs are everywhere. Woof!

MIKE MILLS

Excerpts taken from 'The Making of the Music Video for Pulp's Party Hard'.

Jarvis asked 'well, would you mind if I did some dancing?', and I'm like 'of course not', and [then he said] 'would you mind if they wear T-shirts with dogs on them?' and I'm like, 'course not' and, eh, and that's basically it.

With this whole Pulp thing, when I brought up that idea, Jarvis had this whole tape of this German TV show [*Männer wir kommen!* (1970)], like a German variety show, with really bad keys and this really sort of nasty taste. That was a big input on the video.

There is an internationally known world of bad entertainment brought to you by variety shows all over the world. The first thing Pulp said when they saw the telecine, was like, oh it doesn't look bad enough – that was their big comment – and then we added a little more noise to it.

That's great, can we have more clients like that? We wanted to shoot it on DigiBeta to really make it look like TV [but] the record company wouldn't let us.

This spread:
Video stills from German TV show *Männer wir kommen!* (1970). Costume and set designs by Allen Jones (Production WDR – Westdeutscher Rundfunk, Cologne, West Germany).

Following spread:
Storyboards, 'Party Hard' (1998), Mike Mills.

THE SMASHING CLUB SCENE

Martin Green
2022

Do you remember the first time you heard that news? I certainly do. It was the early hours of Sunday 31st of August 1997 when I drove through St John's Wood and noticed taxis stopped in the streets. It was eerie. I knew something important had happened, so pulled the car over and turned on the radio. The announcer was reporting of a horrific crash in Paris, it was Diana. Everyone was in shock. Only a few minutes before, the mood of that late summer night had been upbeat and positive.

Earlier that evening, I'd been guest DJing during Pulp's Hijack X-FM show – to celebrate the pirate radio station being given a broadcast licence – before driving us to the new cool flat Jarvis had recently moved into on Maida Vale. It was a first-floor apartment, in a small, modernist, 1960s block and below resided the notoriously scathing *Evening Standard* film critic Alexander Walker – who was famously hit over the head on TV with a rolled-up newspaper by an angry Ken Russell. The bachelor pad had once been owned by Tom Jones's and Gilbert O' Sullivan's manager Gordon Mills, who installed a Quadrophonic sound system in the apartment which had remained gloriously unchanged since the 1970s. The design was pure *Persuaders* with a touch of Jason King and a smattering of *New Avengers*. There was a clear Perspex handrail, with chrome supports, that ran along the staircase and an open-plan lounge containing a large chrome cylinder, which revolved to reveal a television and drinks cabinet.

Our love for 1960s and 70s style, music and art was something that bonded and inspired us all during the 90s. Cherry-picking the past was the creative drive behind our scene. This supermarket style was also the approach of my club, 'Smashing', where we would DJ an eclectic mix of Roxy Music, X-Ray Spex, Moroder, Bacharach, Bowie, Blondie, Beck and The Beatles. I was honoured Pulp made our club their weekly home.

Smashing started in 1991 – at the height of Rave – at Maximus in Leicester Square. Host Matthew Glamorre, promoter Adrian Webb, fellow DJ Michael Murphy and I were all bored with the dull monotony of the commercial House club scene. We wanted to start a night with an unpredictable mix of performance, music and mayhem. Within a couple of months, we started to attract like-minded misshapes who also wanted to embark on uncharted disco adventures. Finally, in July 1994, after three years of building a following while travelling around London's most unusual venues, we settled at Eve's Club and our offbeat scene exploded.

Earlier that year, Adrian and I had visited the BBC TV centre to watch Jarvis command an almighty win on Pop Quiz. After the show, we managed to persuade a producer to take us all to the *Blue Peter* garden. We weaved our way through a labyrinth of corridors until finally emerging from the back of the building – and there it was. A children's TV landmark. Our Hallowed Ground. The place where Percy Thrower encouraged us kids to take an interest in urban gardening and wildlife. We sat on a wooden bench humbly admiring Petra's statue and smoked cigarettes like naughty schoolboys.

It was here we excitedly told Jarvis and Steve Mackey about a forgotten hostess club we'd found mothballed beneath a jewellers on Regent Street. We gave them a flyer and then met a week later at our grand opening.

Eve's Club was a 1960s 'Garden of Eden' complete with fibreglass trees, plastic flowers, velvet banquettes, a bamboo bar and an illuminated hydraulic dancefloor which would later appear in the 'Disco 2000' music video and on the cover of the single. Both featured the great-looking young stylist couple Pat and Jo Skinny who Jarvis met, like the cool cast of his 'Common People' video, on the Smashing dancefloor. On Friday nights this underground wonderland would be populated by Indie kids, Mods, Saint Martin's students, Pulp, Blur, Elastica, Oasis, Suede, Minty, Saint Etienne, Denim, Menswear, Earl Brutus, Leigh Bowery, Peter Doig, Jeremy Deller, Gregor Muir, Pam Hogg and Dennis Pennis.

Smashing wasn't just about dancing; it was a social hangout where, at midnight, the music would stop and a show would begin. Sometimes a new band played after a game of musical statues, then host Matthew Glamorre would lead a conga line out of the club and along Regent Street. Each week was full of surprises. Michael Stipe turned up, Keanu Reeves danced to The Stooges and on one especially memorable night after a boisterous Maypole dance, we crowned Courtney Love our May Queen.

The popularity of Smashing grew alongside that of the bands who came down each week. Most of these groups had been part of the indie scene for many years and only very occasionally broke through into the mainstream. But from 1995, things started to change rapidly. Unfortunately labelled with the term Britpop, which no one liked except the tabloid press, groups from the scene stormed the charts and Pulp was no exception. Due to the enormous success of 'Common People', guitarist Mark Webber called and kindly invited me to DJ at shows and after parties on Pulp's forthcoming UK tour. This was October 1995, when 'Disco 2000' was about to be released and was already enjoying tremendous airplay. So, seeing a band who I'd first seen at a small University of London gig becoming massively successful was a thrilling experience. By now even my mum had heard of them.

The tour started in Glasgow Barrowlands and was hugely popular as Pulp knew how to deliver a knockout show – due to years of live performances. As we toured around the UK, audiences grew alongside the band's growing reputation as one of the most original and exciting groups to see. The album *Different Class* was then released in October 1995 and everything went stellar. I continued DJing at their gigs, after parties and record launches. One of the most memorable being for the *This Is Hardcore* album launch, a pink and black themed event held at 'Windows On The World', the glamorous 1970s venue at the top of The Hilton Hotel on Park Lane, held on the 25th of March 1998. The band performed songs from the forthcoming album in the opulent Omar Sharif-style surroundings. Everyone went wild.

Opposite:
Club Smashing, Eve's Club, London
VA6 (pre Add N To (X)).
Photograph by Steven Ball (1995).

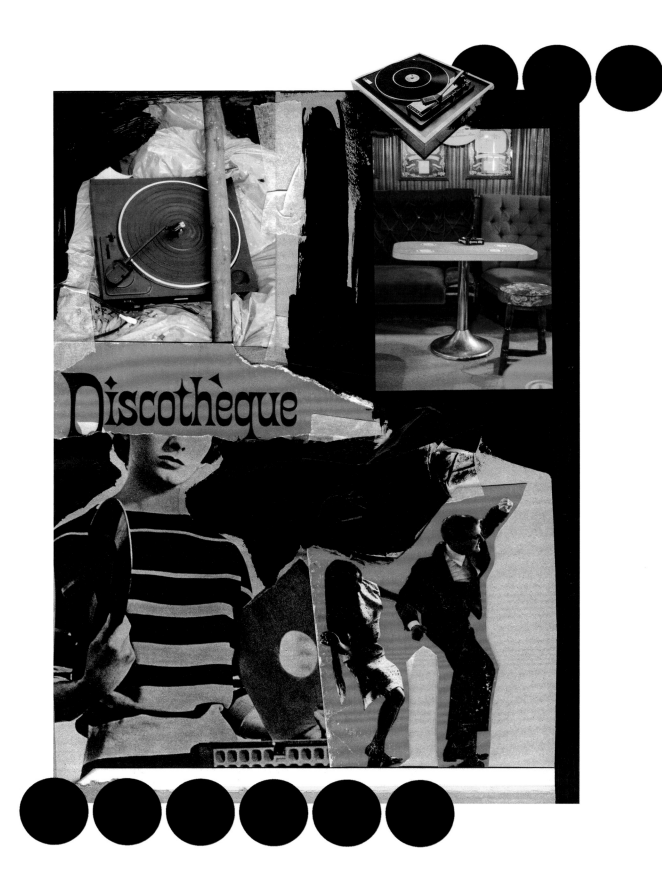

My pre-Spotify DJ playlist during this time included these top-ten floor fillers:
'EVA' – Jean-Jacques Perrey
'Obscene Pornographic Art' – Bongwater
'Money' – Flying Lizards
'Mathar' – The Dave Pike Set
'Psyche Rock' – Pierre Henry
'Beercan' – Beck
'Black Rite' – Mandingo
'Ping Pong' – Stereolab
'Queen Bitch' – David Bowie
'Higher State of Consciousness' – Josh Wink (Tweekin Acid Funk mix)

Before the user-friendly term 'vintage' was devised to make unwanted second-hand goods more palatable, we spent the recession that hit in the early 90s digging around musty charity shops, tatty boot fairs and smelly junk shops looking for clothes, posters, bric-a-brac and records. No one had any money, and these items would inspire and bond us. We spent hours talking about forgotten movies, old TV programmes and rare records – many of which I co-complied onto *The Sound Gallery*, which kick-started the Easy Listening revival in 1995.

As the millennium drew closer, we constantly looked back over the 20th century with an aim to make something modern from our historic discoveries. This artistic approach is beautifully realized in *This Is Hardcore* and especially its title track. The song incorporates the intro of 'Bolero on the Moon Rocks', by Peter Thomas Sound Orchester, from the soundtrack to *Raumpatrouille*, a 1960s German sci-fi cop show. Pulp found this obscure lounge instrumental, looped part of it, then cleverly created a colossus from a simple sample. This is exactly what the 90s was all about – taking the best from the past to forge a new future.

Prior to release, Jarvis gave me a promotional cassette with taster tracks from the forthcoming LP. I used to play it in the car as I drove around the city, blasting out that swaggering opening track as it leapt from the footwell speakers. For me it atmospherically encapsulated a 'now what?' post-Britpop London. Smashing had finished. The beautiful Eve's Club was soon to be demolished. There was a sense that our old West End world was disappearing with property developers swooping in, rents increasing, private members clubs springing up and rich kids arriving in droves. The first half of the 90s was the last time central London was affordable, squats still existed and art college grants were easily obtainable. The song 'This Is Hardcore' is an evocation of foreboding, unease and urban uncertainty, and is as unsettlingly relevant today as it was back then.

Do you remember the first time you heard *This Is Hardcore*? Yes – I do – and it still sounds as original, provocative and non-compromising as it did twenty-five years ago.

PARTY

Unpredictable mix of performance, music and may he...

Electric boogaloo, endless cartwheels, white on red love hearts, stars

HARD
HARD

...aining glitter, hugging a red balloon, POP! sweatbands, spotlights, wind machines

...ke-minded mishapes who also wanted to embark on uncharted disco adventures

EXTRAS

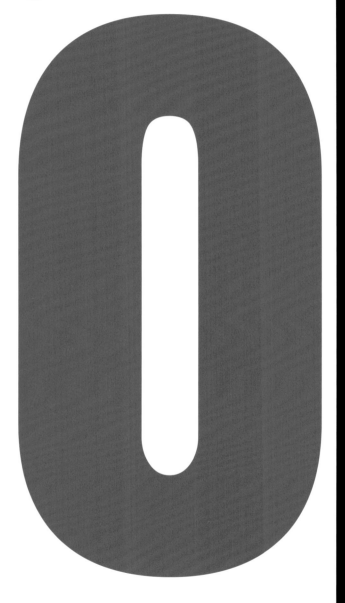

'Like a Friend' video shoot.

Director: Doug Nichol
Produced by: John Moule
Shoot Date: 13 February 1998
Location: Pinewood Studios, London

THIS IS HARDCORE
ALBUM LAUNCH PARTY

HILTON HOTEL

25TH MARCH 1998

This Is Hardcore album launch party.
Date: 25 March 1998
Location: 'Windows on the World Suite' at
the Hilton Hotel, Park Lane, London

Pulp played six songs from the album at the
launch party, including the live debuts of
'Party Hard', 'The Fear' and 'Dishes'. A specially
commissioned short film was shown before Pulp
took to the stage and then DJ Martin Green took
over the decks until 3AM, whilst Pulp-themed
cocktails were served to the audience of over
400 invitees. Guests included Danny Goffey, Neil
Hannon, model Sophie Dahl, Elastica's Donna and
Justin, Massive Attack, Emma Anderson from Lush,
Prodigy's Leeroy, plus television presenters Zoe Ball,
Sara Cox and Jamie Theakston. All guests were
asked to wear black and pink.

Island Records invites you to party hard to launch the Pulp album **THIS IS HARDCORE** 9pm onwards on Wednesday 25th March 1998
at the Windows on the World, Hilton Hotel, Park Lane, London W1. Entrance only via rear lobby on Hertford Road.

Dress code: Black and pink. This ticket is strictly non transferable.

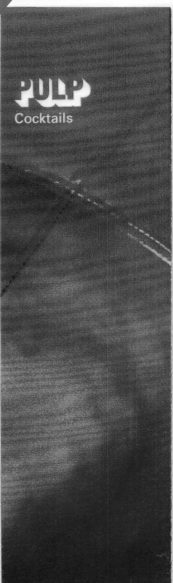

PULP

Cocktails

Ksenia
Vodka, tomato juice, lemon juice, Tabasco
Worcestershire sauce

John Huntley
Vodka, cranberry, lime juice

Jan-Marie
Vodka, Midori, orange juice, sweet 'n' sour

Beverly
Vodka, Galliano, orange juice

Pheline
Vodka, Sweet n Sour, Ginger Beer

Seductive Barry
Vodka, Midori, Pineapple Juice

Hardcordial
Vodka, Cranberry Juice, Grapefruit Juice

The Professional
Vodka, Orange Juice

John Currin
Vodka, Dry Vermouth

Peter Saville
Flavoured Vodka, Dry Vermouth

Party Hard
Vodka, Lime Juice, Sugar Syrup, Soda Water

The Laughing Boy
Vodka, Apple Juice

The Tipsy
Vodka, Grapefruit Juice

End Of The Line
Vodka, Cranberry Juice, Peach Schnapps

SMIRNOFF

PULP
THIS IS
HARDCORE
LAUNCH PARTY
MARCH 25TH 1998
UNRESTRICTED
UNCENSORED
WORKING ACTION
XXX

FINSBURY PARK

LIVE SHOW

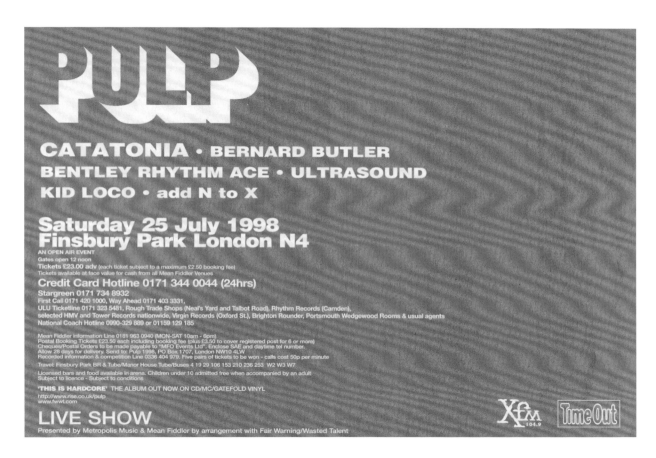

Finsbury Park 'Live Show' concert.
Date: 25 July 1998
Location: Finsbury Park, London

Pulp held their own one-day festival in Finsbury Park. It was the first headline Pulp concert in the UK since the *This Is Hardcore* album had been released. The support bands were Catatonia, Bernard Butler, Bentley Rhythm Ace, Ultrasound, Kid Loco and Add N To (X). The concert was filmed and released later in 1998 on the official 'The Park is Mine' video.

RESTRICTED

This Is Hardcore Saudi Arabian cassette release. Cover model Ksenia Zlobina has been replaced with male model/actor, John Huntley. All references to 'Hardcore' and 'Seductive' have been deleted from the inlay card as have most of the images.

CENSORED

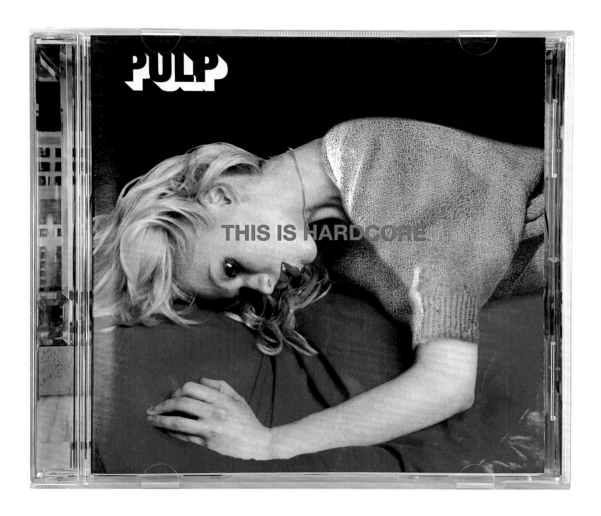

This Is Hardcore Malaysian CD release, with custom censored sleeve artwork. A gold knitted jumper was added in Photoshop to the cover model, Ksenia Zlobina.

END
07
CREDITS

THANK YOU

In memory of Steve Mackey (1966–2023)

Jarvis Cocker / Nick Banks / Candida Doyle / Steve Mackey / Mark Webber

Russell Senior

Jeannette Lee, Geoff Travis and all at
Rough Trade Management.

Special thanks to Giles Bosworth at
Acrylic Afternoons, founded in 1997 to celebrate,
promote and archive the work of Pulp.
acrylicafternoons.com

Original 35mm negatives and transparencies
scanned by the good people at Take It Easy Lab,
a mail-order film-processing lab in Leeds.
takeiteasylab.com

HARDCORE TIMELINE

1996

October
Pulp begin to write songs for their next album, *This Is Hardcore*.
December
Jarvis Cocker on the front cover of GQ 'The Great British Issue'.
December–January
Jarvis Cocker is in New York.

1997

January–December
Further song writing and recording at Olympic Studios.
20 January
Russell Senior's departure from Pulp is announced.
8 April
Microsoft releases the Internet Explorer 4 Beta.
1 May
The UK General Election, Tony Blair becomes Prime Minister.
29 August
Netflix is founded by Marc Randolph and Reece Hastings as an online DVD rental service.
30 August
The first radio broadcast of 'Help the Aged' on Xfm.
31 August
Princess Diana dies at 36, in a car crash in Paris.
6 September
The funeral of Diana, Princess of Wales.
16 October
Pulp perform a DJ set at HMV on Oxford Street, London.
17–19 October
The 'Help the Aged' video shoot takes place at Stoke Newington Town Hall and White City.
20 October
Shaken and Stirred: The David Arnold James Bond Project released ('All Time High').
31 October
La Monte Young/Marian Zazeela Benefit Concert at Barbican Hall, London.
7 November
Pulp perform 'Help the Aged' on BBC One's Top of the Pops.

11 November
The release of the 'Help the Aged' single.
14 November
Pulp appear on Channel 4's TFI Friday.
21 November
Pulp perform a second performance of 'Help the Aged' on BBC One's *Top of the Pops*.
25–27 November
Pulp takeover of the John Peel Show with Geoff Travis and Martin Green.
8–14 December
An interview with David Bowie about smoking by Jarvis Cocker appears in *The Big Issue*.
December
'Help the Aged' rated 12th best single of the year in *Melody Maker* and 41st best single of the year by *NME*.
December
Photography for the new album is completed.

1998

9 January
The final day of recording for the *This Is Hardcore* album.
30 January
A new film adaptation of *Great Expectations* is released, featuring the Pulp song 'Like A Friend'.
10–13 February
The 'This is Hardcore' video shoot takes place at Pinewood Studios, along with the filming of the Hardcore documentary.
13 February
The 'Like A Friend' video shoot takes place at Pinewood Studios.
9 March
The release of the 'This is Hardcore' single.
15 March
Part one of the BBC Radio 1 Pulp documentary airs.
22 March
Part two of the BBC Radio 1 Pulp documentary airs, along with first-time plays of *This Is Hardcore* songs.
25 March
The album launch party for *This Is Hardcore* at the Hilton Hotel, London, with a private performance.
27 March
Pulp perform 'This is Hardcore' on BBC One's Top of the Pops.
30 March
The release of the *This Is Hardcore* album.

5 April
This Is Hardcore reaches number one in the UK album charts, having sold just over 50,000 copies in its first week. It reaches the top ten in France and Norway and top twenty in Australia, Japan and Sweden.
17 April
This Is Hardcore is certified Gold (sales of 100,000 copies) by the BPI.
23–24 April
The 'A Little Soul' video shoot takes place at Olympic Studios, London.
24 April
The documentary about 'A Little Soul' is filmed at Olympic Studios, London.
1 May
Pulp perform 'The Fear', 'Dishes' and 'This Is Hardcore' on the BBC's Later... with Jools Holland.
5 June
Pulp perform 'A Little Soul' on Channel 4's TFI Friday.
8 June
The release of 'A Little Soul' as a single.
19 June
Pulp perform 'A Little Soul' on BBC One's Top of the Pops.

USA and Canada tour.
   9 June
   Paradise Club, Boston, USA.
   10 June
   Massey Hall, Toronto, Canada.
   13 June
   Performance of 'Party Hard' on NBC's Late Night with Conan O'Brien Show, New York, USA.
   13 June
   9.30 Club, Washington DC, USA.
   15 June
   Pulp attend a signing session at Tower Records, New York, USA.
   16 June
   Hammerstein Ballroom, New York, USA.

European festival tour.
   20 June
   Rockpalast Festival, Loreley, Germany.
   21 June
   Hurricane Festival, Germany.
   26 June
   St Gallen Festival, Switzerland.
   27 June
   Roskilde Festival, Denmark.

28 June
Glastonbury Festival, UK.
1 July
Imperial Festival, Portugal.
2 July
Midtfyns Festival, Denmark.
3 July
Torhout Festival, Belgium.
4 July
Werchter Festival, Belgium.
5 July
Les Eurockéennes Festival, Belfort,
France.
10 July
Dr Music Festival, Spain.
11 July
Galway Big Day Out, Ireland.
12 July
T in the Park, Scotland.
16 July
Rockwave Festival, Greece.
19 July
Forest Glade Festival, Austria.
23 July
Skansen Park, Stockholm.
25 July
Finsbury Park, London.

July
Jarvis's yellow Hillman Imp car is crushed
into a cube at Mayer Parry Recycling Ltd.,
Willesden (now EMR Ltd) and given away
to Pulp fan Bridget Booth after a Pulp
People competition.
28 July
Mercury Music Prize shortlist announced.
This Is Hardcore one of 10 albums of
the year.
7 August
The 'Party Hard' video shoot takes place
at Asylum Studios, Perivale.
September
Pulp write new songs at Monnow Valley
Studios, Wales.
7 September
The release of 'Party Hard' as a single.
11 September
Pulp perform 'Party Hard' on Channel 4's
TFI Friday.
14 September
The reissue of *This Is Hardcore* as
extended CD with 'This Is Glastonbury'
bonus disc.
18 September
Pulp perform 'Party Hard' on BBC One's
Top of the Pops.
16 September
The Mercury Music Prize, *This Is Hardcore*
nominated but Best Album won by

Gomez, for *Bring It On*.
19 September
Jarvis turns 35.
23 October
The film *Velvet Goldmine* is released,
featuring 'We Are The Boyz' in
the soundtrack.
23 November
'The Park is Mine' released on VHS.
Cover design by Fly (Fabian
Monheim and Sophia Wood).
Photography by Paul Burgess.

Japan tour.
18 September
Akasaka Blitz, Tokyo.
20 September
On Air East, Tokyo.
21 September
Liquid Room, Tokyo.
22 September
Imperial Hall, Osaka.

Australia and New Zealand tour.
25 September
Metropolis, Perth, Australia.
27 September
Festival Hall, Melbourne, Australia.
28 September
Enmore Theatre, Sydney, Australia.
29 September
Enmore Theatre, Sydney, Australia.
30 September
Enmore Theatre, Sydney, Australia.
2 October
Thebarton Theatre, Adelaide, Australia.
3 October
Livid Festival, Brisbane, Australia.
5 October
North Shore Events Centre, Auckland,
New Zealand.
23 October
Collaborative concert with Terry Riley,
Jarvis, Mark and Steve at Barbican
Hall, London.

UK Arena tour.
17 November
Hereford Leisure Centre.
19 November
Wembley Arena, London.
21 November
Royal Court Theatre, Liverpool.
22 November
Apollo, Manchester.
23 November
Apollo, Manchester.
25 November
Trentham Gardens, Stoke-on-Trent.

26 November
Doncaster Dome.
28 November
Hull Arena.
29 November
SECC, Glasgow.
30 November
Cardiff International Arena.
2 December
NEC, Birmingham.
3 December
Brighton Centre.
5 December
Bournemouth International Centre.

1999

11 January
The All Seeing I's 'Walk Like a Panther'
single released.
16, 23 February, 3 March
'Journeys into the Outside' (dir. Martin
Wallace) with Jarvis Cocker is broadcast
on UK television in three episodes.
26 April
The Ivor Novello Awards nominations are
announced. 'A Little Soul' nominated
for Best Song Musically and Lyrically
alongside 'C'est La Vie' by B*Witched
and 'Believe' by Cher.
27 May
The Ivor Novello Awards ceremony. Cher
wins the best song award for 'Believe'.
10 June
Venice – Palazzo Pisani Moretta – 48th
Venice Biennale Private Party for British
artist and exhibitor Gary Hume. Pulp
all wore polo neck sweaters and played
behind a Venetian blind.
2 July
Jarvis contributes to Hal Willner's 'The
Harry Smith Project', the final event of
Nick Cave's Meltdown Festival, at the
Royal Festival Hall, London. Jarvis played
two traditional American folk/blues
songs, backed by Mark Webber on guitar
plus the house band.
31 August
The Quiet Revolution, Flux Festival
Queen's Hall, Edinburgh, Scotland.
2 September
Liss Ard Festival, Ireland.
30 November
Glass Harmonica Gig, featuring Jarvis
Cocker, Steve Mackey and Alasdair Malloy,
at Mother Bar, 333 Club, London.
31 December
New Year's Eve and the end of the century.

IMAGE CREDITS

p.3 Title page – graphic image by Alexa Vieira.

01. PRELUDE

p.4 Pulp Box of Wonders. Paul Burgess (2023).

p.8 Photograph of Steve Mackey, Paul Burgess and Jarvis Cocker by Jeannette Lee. Pinewood Studios (Feb 1998)

p.10 & 11 Pulp group montage for Hardcore tour booklet 'The Professional' by Paul Burgess and Trevor Dickinson (1998).

p.12 & 12 Jarvis's shoes photographed by Paul Burgess (1998).

p.14 Abstracted (one hundred frames) film still image of 35mm film loop by Louise Colbourne made using the No.W.here film lab rostrum camera (2012). Original photograph by A.F.J Colbourne of Sheila Sanderson in 1963.

p.17 Jarvis's shoes photographed by Paul Burgess (Pinewood studios 1998).

p.18 Photograph of *This Is Hardcore* album cover taken at author's home by Paul Burgess. Model – Ksenia Zlobina. Art Direction by John Currin and Peter Saville. Photography by Horst Diekgerdes. Design by Howard Wakefield and Paul Hetherington. Casting by Sascha Behrendt. Styling by Camille Bidault-Waddington.

p.20 & 21 Photograph of Nick Banks at the Hilton Hotel by Horst Diekgerdes. Design by Howard Wakefield and Paul Hetherington. Art Direction by John Currin and Peter Saville.

p.22 Picture of Jarvis in Pinewood dressing room taken by Paul Burgess using a 3D camera.

p.24 'Twinned' 2021. Photography and collage by Paul Burgess.

p.27 'Mal' 2022. Photography and collage by Paul Burgess.

02. THIS IS HARDCORE

All photography by Paul Burgess unless otherwise stated.

p.30 to 41 *This Is Hardcore* promotional video on set and in the dressing room.

p.42 Type arrangement by Louise Colbourne.

p.43 'Filmstrips' collage by Paul Burgess (2022).

p.44 & 45 Jarvis Cocker and Steve Mackey in the dressing room at Pinewood studios. Photograph by Paul Burgess (Feb 1998).

p.46 & 47 A still from *The Fuzzy Pink Nightgown*, United Artists, 1957. Jane Russell.
From the book *Still Life* by Diane Keaton & Marvin Heiferman. Callaway Editions 1983. Image arrangement by Louise Colbourne.

p.48 Jan Marie von Giebelhausen and Steve Mackey. 'This Is Hardcore' video shoot. Photograph by Paul Burgess (Feb 1998).

p.49 Steve Mackey top and Jan Marie von Giebelhausen bottom. Film transparency strip sequence serendipity. This Is Hardcore video shoot. Photograph by Paul Burgess (Feb 1998).

p.50 & 51 Dancers – 'This Is Hardcore' video shoot. Image arrangement by Louise Colbourne. Photographs by Paul Burgess (Feb 1998).

p.52 & 53 Dancers – 'This Is Hardcore' video shoot. Photograph by Paul Burgess (Feb 1998).

p.54 & 55 Steve Mackey and Jarvis Cocker – 'This Is Hardcore' video shoot. Photography and montage by Paul Burgess.

p.56 Mark Webber – 'This Is Hardcore' video shoot. Photograph by Paul Burgess (Feb 1998).

p.58 & 59 'This Is Hardcore' film set. Pinewood Studios. Photograph by Paul Burgess (Feb 1998).

p.60 & 61 Nick Banks – 'This Is Hardcore' film set. Pinewood Studios. Photograph by Paul Burgess (Feb 1998).

p.62. Jarvis's shoes – 'This Is Hardcore' video shoot. Photograph by Paul Burgess (Feb 1998).

p.63. Extra in chair – 'This Is Hardcore' video shoot. Photograph by Paul Burgess (Feb 1998).

p.64 *Still Life* book cover. Diane Keaton & Marvin Heiferman. Callaway Editions 1983.

p.66. Jarvis Cocker – 'This Is Hardcore' video shoot. Photograph by Paul Burgess (Feb 1998).

p.67 A still from *Cast a Giant Shadow*, United Artists, 1966. Angie Dickinson and Kirk Douglas. From the book *Still Life* by Diane Keaton & Marvin Heiferman. Callaway Editions 1983.

p.68 & 69 'This Is Hardcore' – Treatment story by Doug Nichol (Dec 1997). Original fax.

p.70 Jarvis Cocker screen test. Pinewood studios. Photograph by Paul Burgess (Feb 1998).

p.71 'This Is Hardcore' – Treatment story (continued) by Doug Nichol (Dec 1997). Original fax.

p.72. Major Set Scenes – 'This Is Hardcore' – Pinewood studios. Text by Mark Tanner, Art Director.

P.73 Left to right – Dancers – 'This Is Hardcore' video shoot. Doug Nichol's original clapper board. Mark Webber and Jan Marie von Giebelhausen. Jarvis Cocker: 'This Is Hardcore' documentary flyer 'Ya Mo Be There'. Photographs by Paul Burgess (Feb 1998).

p.74 & 75 Set photographs by Mark Tanner (top left / bottom right). On set photographs (bottom left / top right) by Paul Burgess .

p.76 Ksenia Zlobina and Jarvis Cocker – 'This Is Hardcore' video shoot. Photograph by Paul Burgess (Feb 1998).

p.77 Jan Marie von Giebelhausen and Nick Banks. 'This Is Hardcore' video shoot. Photograph by Paul Burgess (Feb 1998)

p.78 John Stezaker, 'Opening II' (1994). Courtesy of The Approach.

p.79 Candida Doyle – 'This Is Hardcore' video shoot. Photograph by Paul Burgess (Feb 1998).

p.80 & 81 John Stezaker, *Untitled* (1985). Courtesy of The Approach.

p.82 & 83 Jarvis Cocker – 'This Is Hardcore' video shoot. Photographs by Paul Burgess (Feb 1998).

p.84 to 88 Sergei Sviatchenko, *Less* collage series (2022).

p.89 Candida Doyle – in hair curlers. 'This Is Hardcore' video shoot dressing room. Photograph by Paul Burgess (Feb 1998).

p.90 Candida Doyle 'This Is Hardcore' video shoot. Photograph by Paul Burgess (Feb 1998).

p.91 Jarvis Cocker – 'This Is Hardcore' video shoot. Photograph by Paul Burgess (Feb 1998).

03. HELP THE AGED

All photography by Paul Burgess taken on the set of the 'Help the Aged' video shoot. White City Studio, Silver Road, London (unless otherwise stated) 17–18 October 1997.

p.94 John Currin, *The Neverending Story*, 1994. Ink on paper, 53.0 x 45.2 x 3.8 cm. Courtesy of Sadie Coles Gallery.

04. A LITTLE SOUL

05. PARTY HARD

p.187 Mark Webber, Steve Mackey and Candida Doyle. 'Party Hard' video shoot. Asylum Studios. Photograph by Paul Burgess (Aug 1998).

p.189 Jarvis Cocker with balloon. 'Party Hard' video shoot. Asylum Studios. Photograph by Paul Burgess (Aug 1998).

p.190 & 191 Jarvis Cocker filmed against green screen. 'Party Hard' video shoot. Asylum Studios. Photographs by Paul Burgess (Aug 1998).

p.192 Jarvis Cocker, Candida Doyle and Martin Green at the BBC for the John Peel Takeover. Photograph by Mark Webber (Nov 1997).

p.194 Club Smashing, Eve's Club, London. VA6 (pre Add N To (X). Photograph by Steven Ball (1995).

p.196 *Discothèque* collage by Paul Burgess (2022).

p.200 & 201 Dancers: 'Party Hard' video shoot. Asylum Studios. Photograph by Paul Burgess (Aug 1998).

06. EXTRAS

All photographs by Paul Burgess (unless otherwise stated).

p.203 Jarvis Cocker and Candida Doyle. 'Like a Friend' video shoot. Photograph by Paul Burgess (Feb 1998).

p.204–215 'Like a Friend' video shoot, Pinewood Studios. Photographs by Paul Burgess (Feb 1998). Image arrangement and graphics by Louise Colbourne.

p.216 & 217 Photograph from the Hilton Hotel window by Horst Diekgerdes for *This Is Hardcore* album cover (1998). Design by Howard Wakefield and Paul Hetherington. Art Direction by John Currin and Peter Saville.

p.218 & 219 Invite and cocktail list from the *This Is Hardcore* album launch party at the Hilton Hotel (25 March 1998).

P.220 & 221 Main photograph of Jarvis by Nicky Haycock. Audience photographs by Paul Burgess. Party laminate courtesy of Martin Green.

p.222 & 223 Photographs by Nicky Haycock. *This Is Hardcore* album launch party at the Hilton Hotel (25 March 1998) Montage by Paul Burgess (2023).

p.224 & 225 Images from the *This Is Hardcore* album launch party at the Hilton Hotel. Photographs by Paul Burgess (25 March 1998).

p.226 Pulp badge. Photograph by Paul Burgess (1998).

p.227 Pulp Finsbury Park Live Show. 25 July 1998.

p.228 & 229 Jarvis Cocker. Pulp Live Show, Finsbury Park. 25 July 1998. Photograph by Paul Burgess.

p.230 Pulp fans. Finsbury Park. 25 July 1998. Photographs by Paul Burgess.

p.231 Jarvis Cocker. Finsbury Park. 25 July 1998. Photograph by Paul Burgess.

p.232 & 233 Pulp onstage with Richard Hawley. Finsbury Park. 25 July 1998. Photographs by Paul Burgess.

p.234 & 235 Pulp backstage and Finsbury Park audience scenes. Top right image: Zoë Miller, Mark Webber and Dominique Miller. Bottom right: Dominique Miller and Mark Webber. Couple with the Pulp bag: Sheila and Tony Webber.

p.236 Competition winners meeting Pulp backstage. Finsbury Park. 25 July 1998. Photographs by Paul Burgess.

p.237 Pulp merchandise stall. Pulp fans in front of stage. Finsbury Park. 25 July 1998. Photographs by Paul Burgess. Photograph of *This Is Hardcore* promo bed sheets courtesy of Giles Bosworth at Acrylic Afternoons.

p.238 & 239 *This Is Hardcore* cassette and CD courtesy of Giles Bosworth at Acrylic Afternoons.

p.240 Left: DJ Jarvis Cocker at Mark Webber's Little Stabs at Happiness, Scala, London, 17 April 1999. Fist in the air, Dominique Miller. Right: Pat and Jo Skinny. 'A Little Soul' video shoot. Olympic Studios. Photographs by Paul Burgess.

p.241 Top to bottom: Pulp (rehearsal studio), Zoë Miller, Steve Mackey and Jeannette Lee, Jarvis and Antony Genn, Glastonbury Festival 1998. Jarvis singing 'Saturday Night' by Whigfield at Keith Allen's Karaoke event.

p.244 & 245 Pulp: group photo. 'Like a Friend' video shoot. Pinewood studios. Photograph by Paul Burgess (Feb 1998).

p. 246 & 247 Jarvis Cocker: 'Party Hard' video shoot. Asylum Studios. Photograph by Paul Burgess (Aug 1998).

CONTRIBUTOR BIOGRAPHIES

Paul Burgess is a designer, photographer and author. He was Principal Lecturer for the Illustration programme at the University of Brighton from 2005 to 2020 and studied at Camberwell School of Art and the Royal College of Art. Burgess is also a collage artist and his work has been featured in many UK and international publications and exhibitions.

Louise Colbourne is an artist, designer and educator. She also works as an independent creative director and is currently course leader for MA Graphic Design at the University of Brighton.

Jarvis Cocker has been Pulp's vocalist since he started the group in 1978. He is also a musician, broadcaster and best-selling author.

John Currin is an American painter based in New York City. He is best known for his satirical figurative paintings. Currin was the art director, alongside Peter Saville, on the *This Is Hardcore* (1998) album sleeve and the 'Help the Aged' (1997) music video.

Horst Diekgerdes is a German photographer who started his professional career in Paris before moving to London. Working in fashion and music across Europe, America and Asia. Horst took the photographs for the *This Is Hardcore* album sleeve and the singles 'Party Hard, 'This Is Hardcore' and 'A Little Soul'.

Candida Doyle has been Pulp's keyboard player since joining the group in 1984. Her brother, Magnus Doyle, was Pulp's drummer between 1983 to 1986. Doyle is the daughter of actress Sandra Voe and actor, writer and director Rex Doyle.

Martin Green is a music collector, DJ and art curator. Co-founder of Club Smashing and Duovision Arts. He compiled the album *The Sound Gallery* in 1995, with Patrick Whitaker and Tristram Penna. Martin was Pulp's go-to DJ for many events and after-show parties, and still DJs with Jarvis Cocker to this day.

Florian Habicht is regarded as one of New Zealand's most distinctive filmmakers. Habicht makes films his own way, using small crews, often experimenting and collaborating with close friends. Florian directed the film *Pulp: a Film About Life, Death & Supermarkets* (2014).

Garth Jennings is an English director, screenwriter and actor. Films he has directed include *The Hitchhiker's Guide to the Galaxy* (2005), *Son of Rambow* (2007), *Sing* (2016), and *Sing 2* (2021). He co-founded the music video production company Hammer & Tongs alongside Nick Goldsmith and they directed the Pulp music videos 'Help the Aged' (1997) and 'A Little Soul'(1998).

Jackson Ellis Leach is a professional session drummer. He played the young Jarvis in the music video for 'A Little Soul'.

Doug Nichol is an American film director and a three-time Grammy Award winner and nominee. Nichol started out his career making music videos and documentaries for the likes of Sting, Lenny Kravitz, Madonna, and Aerosmith. He has directed hundreds of commercials for brands such as Levi's, Mercedes, Smirnoff, Virgin and Ford. His film *California Typewriter*, featuring Tom Hanks, Sam Shepard and John Mayer, was released in 2016. He directed the Pulp music video for 'This Is Hardcore'.

Stephen Mallinder is an artist, academic and musician who was a founding member of the group Cabaret Voltaire and is currently a member of both Wrangler and Creep Show. Mallinder was born and raised in the city of Sheffield.

Mike Mills is an American film and music video director, writer and graphic designer. He is best known for his independent films, *Beginners* (2010), *20th Century Women* (2016), for which he received an Academy Award for Best Original Screenplay nomination, and *C'mon, C'mon* (2021). He directed the Pulp music video 'Party Hard'(1998).

Peter Saville is a world-renowned art director and graphic designer. He produced many record sleeves for artists signed to Factory Records including Joy Division, New Order and Suede. Saville has worked with many fashion brands. He ran his own studio Peter Saville Associates and, later, a design studio with Howard Wakefield called 'The Apartment'. Saville art directed the album sleeve for *This Is Hardcore*, alongside John Currin.

Jo and Pat Skinny worked with Pulp as stylists on many occasions during the 1990s. As a couple they starred in the music video for 'Disco 2000' (1995). Pat Skinny is also one of the 'bearded men' in the video for 'Help the Aged'.

John Stezaker is a conceptual artist who works with collage. He studied at the Slade School of Art. Stezaker also worked as a tutor at both Central St Martins and the Royal College of Art, teaching Jarvis Cocker when he was a student at Central St Martins.

Sergei Sviatchenko is a Danish-Ukrainian architect, artist, photographer and curator. He is a representative of the Ukrainian New Wave that arose in Ukraine throughout the 1980s. Sviatchenko is creative director of the Less Festival of Collage, Viborg and Just A Few Works. He has lived in Denmark since the 1990s.

Mark Tanner is a production designer with over forty years of experience working in film and TV across Europe, USA and South Africa. Mark was the production designer/art director who designed the various set designs for the 'This Is Hardcore' (1998) music video.

Howard Wakefield has created campaigns for celebrated musicians and identities, and advertising for numerous global brands. He has designed record sleeves for New Order, Joy Division, Goldie, Pulp, Suede and others. Howard was a founding member of Peter Saville Associates and currently runs a studio with Sarah Parris, called Colour & Form. Howard designed the record cover and marketing material for *This Is Hardcore* and for the singles 'Party Hard', 'This Is Hardcore' and 'A Little Soul' along with co-designer Paul Hetherington.

VIDEO SHOOT INFORMATION

HELP THE AGED

Director: Hammer & Tongs
Art Director: John Currin
Produced by: Nick Goldsmith
Shoot Date: 17–18 October 1997
Locations: Stoke Newington Town Hall ('stair lift and old people's home' scenes); White City Studio, Silver Road, London (green-screen 'space' scenes)

THIS IS HARDCORE

Production Company: Partizan Midi-Minuit
Director: Doug Nichol
Shoot Date: 10–13th February 1998
Location: Pinewood Studios (L&C Stages) Pinewood Road, Iver, Bucks, SL0 0NH

Some of the actors' dialogue at the beginning of the video is taken from the film Written on the Wind *directed by Douglas Sirk in 1956.*

The music video features This Is Hardcore *album cover model Ksenia Zlobina (originally from Belarus and aged 18 at the time of the photoshoot) and Jan Marie von Giebelhausen as the woman dancing in the bedroom (an American model of Czech origin and today a designer in her own right based in Australia).*

Production: Partizan Midi-Minuit
Commissioner: Emma Davis at Island
Director: Doug Nichol
Executive Producer: Pete Chambers
Producer: John Moule
Production Manager: Tim Kerrison
1st Assistant: Lucas Harding
2nd Assistant: Chris Marshall
Production Assistant: Geraldine Geraghty
Director of Photography: Joe Zizzo
Focus Puller: Olivier Greco
Loader: Marcus Domleo
Colour Grading: Jean-Clément Soret
Art Director: Mark Tanner
Assistant Art Director: Ravi
Set Stylist: Marina Morris
Construction Manager: Paul Warwick
Standby Painter: Bruce Gallup
Scenic Artist: James Hunt

Standby Carpenter: Chris Hartney
Props Master: Maurice Jones
SFX Master: Ross King
Costume Designer: Sammy Howarth
Assistant Stylist: Charlotte Couchman
Assistant Stylist: Michael Mooney
Make-Up: Louise Constad
Make-Up Assistant: Carol Morley
Hair: Lisa Laudant
Hair Assistant: Charlotte Murray
Grip: Tony Sankey
Gaffer (1st Unit): Jim Knight
Spark: Dave McWinny
Spark: Mike Parker
Spark: Mike Chambers
Gaffer (2nd Unit): Ashley Palin
Spark: Tim Willey
Spark: Enrico De Santio
Spark: Mark Ward
Rigger: Dave Broadfoot
Playback/Sound Rec: Steve Barnacle
Offline Editor: Tony Kearns
Runner: Kim Moore
Runner: James Mackay
Runner: Grant Lucking
Runner: Nina Fox
Catering: Eat to the Beat

LIKE A FRIEND

Director: Doug Nichol
Produced by: John Moule
Shoot Date: 13 February 1998
Location: Pinewood Studios, London

Filmed at Pinewood, at the end of the This Is Hardcore shoot, on the same revolving stage used for the 'Busby Berkely' scene. The song was written specifically for inclusion in the Alfonso Cuarón film Great Expectations.

All members of Pulp were in high spirits during the filming, Jarvis messing around, playing Nick's drum kit, dancing with Candida, breakdancing. The group letting off steam after an intense week shooting 'This Is Hardcore'. Rough video footage was filmed on set with a camcorder by Paul Burgess, which later appeared in the 'Home Movies' section of the Pulp 'Hits' DVD released in 2002.

A LITTLE SOUL

Director: Hammer & Tongs / Garth Jennings
Produced by: Nick Goldsmith
Shoot Date: 23–24 April 1998
Location: Olympic Studios (Studio One), 117 Church Road, Barnes, London, SW13 9HL

A behind-the-scenes documentary film was made on 24 April 1998 on set at Olympic Studios by Paul Burgess and Litsa Aris. Jarvis wrote out 46 questions related to the themes of the Hardcore album, and these questions were put to the child actors, make-up artist, stylists, canteen staff and the director. The 16mm film remains unseen at the time of writing.

Child Actors:
Little Jarvis: Jackson Ellis Leach
Little Steve: Marc Vambe
Little Mark: Jack Straw
Little Nick: Jackson Milner
Little Candida: Ellice Cundall

Director: Hammer & Tongs (Garth Jennings)
Producer: Nick Goldsmith
Production Manager: Pippa Harrison
Production Assistant: Mrs Zoe Al-Kubaisi
First Assistant Director: Griffin
Second Assistant Director: Mark Jackson
Commissioner: Emma Davis
Runner: Little Lou Cooper
Runner: Rob Tyler
Lighting Cameraman: Dan Landin
Focus Puller: Federico Alfonzo
Clapper Loader: John Mitchell
Gaffer: Matthew Moffit
Electrician: Paul Sharp
Electrician: Harry Wiggins
Electrician: John Corbett
Grip: Ron Nicholls
Playback: Richard Undrell
Art Director: Joel Collins
Assistant Art Director: Katie Millward
Make-Up: Gina Kane
Make-Up Assistant: Denise Carol
Stylists: Pat & Jo Skinny
Casting Director for child actors: Sue Pocklington (Murder My Darlings)
Catering: Cath's Café

PARTY HARD

Director: Mike Mills
Produced by: Nick Landon
Shoot Date: 7th August 1998
Location: Asylum Studios, Studio 1, 1 Wadsworth Close, Perivale, Middlesex, UB6 7DG
Dancers (Pineapple Dance Agency): Rachel Parry, Selina Charlier, Stephanie Fortescue, Amy Pearson, Anna Leigh, Jayne Hardy, Lisa Clare Yovell, Stephanie Miller, Melanie Everett, Teresa Lambert, Emma Boardman, Katie Sarah Colinge, Vivienne Clarke, Sarah Impey

Dancers (Success Dance Agency): Kristijana, Christy, Anna McDonald

Choreographer: Carol Fletcher

Production Company: Serious Pictures
Director: Mike Mills
Producer: Nick Landon
Director of Photography: Adrian Wild
Assistant Director: Ben Gill
Production Manager: Richard Weager
Production Assistant: Ben Sullivan
Focus Puller: J.P. Seresin
Clapper Loader: Charlie Woodburn
B Cam Operator: Alan Stewart
B Cam Focus Puller: Tammo Van Hoorn
Grip: Rick Woollard
Gaffer: Gary Owen
Sparks: Geoff Burlingson
Sparks: Robin Brigham
Sparks: Brian Miller
Rigger: Dave Harrison
Art Director: Roger Swanborough
Art Dept Assistant: Katrina Andrews
Stylists: Pat & Jo Skinny
Make Up: Fay Leith
Make Up Assistant: Joanne Byrne
Make Up Assistant: Emma Williams
Hair: Matt Raine c/o Children of Vision
Hair Assistant: Selina Ream
Playback: Quillan Larratt
Runner: Simon Pattullo
Runner: Patrick Evans
Runner: Richard Hall
Casting: Layton & Norcliffe Casting
Caterers: Eat Your Hearts Out

Huge thanks to:
Doug Nichol, Mike Mills, Garth Jennings, Florian Habicht, John Currin, Peter Saville, Howard Wakefield, Horst Diekgerdes, Mark Tanner, Candida Doyle, Martin Green, Stephen Mallinder, John Stezaker, The Approach, Sergei Sviatchenko, Jeannette Lee, Mark Webber, Giles Bosworth, Jane Savidge, Young Kim, Jo and Pat Skinny, Zoë Miller, Glen Johnson, Sadie Coles, Elfyn Round, Alexa Vieira, Steven Ball, Litsa Aris, Ian Dickson, Peter Anderson, Jackson Ellis Leach, Paul Gorman, Trevor Dickinson, Nicky Haycock, Lily Rose Dawes, Rose Walker at the Letterpress facility, School of Art and Media, University of Brighton, Callum Round, Walter Burgess, Darren Wall, Lucas Dietrich, Beth Siveyer, Evie Tarr. . . and not forgetting Alex Deck from Pulp People.

Pulp-related books:
Pulp's This Is Hardcore
by Jane Savidge. 33 1/3 Series (2024)
I'm with Pulp, Are You?
by Mark Webber (2023)
And it Started There: From Punk to Pulp
by Nick Banks (2023)
Good Pop, Bad Pop
by Jarvis Cocker (2022)
Freak Out the Squares
by Russell Senior (2015)
Mother, Brother, Lover: Selected Lyrics
by Jarvis Cocker (2011)
Uncommon: An Essay on Pulp
by Owen Hatherley (2011)
Truth and Beauty: the Story of Pulp
by Mark Sturdy (2003)
Pulp by Martin Aston (1996)

Pulp-related websites:
acrylicafternoons.com
pulpwiki.net
feelingcalledlive.co.uk
baritalia.activeboard.com
jarviscocker.net
markwebber.org.uk
stevemackeystudio.com
pulpsongs.wordpress.com

Pulp-related social media:
@welovepulp
@jarvisbransoncocker
@steve_mackey
@therealnickbank
@imwithpulp